THE
DOLL'S HOUSE

Marie Swift

authorHOUSE®

AuthorHouse™ UK Ltd.
500 Avebury Boulevard
Central Milton Keynes, MK9 2BE
www.authorhouse.co.uk
Phone: 08001974150

This book is printed on acid-free paper.

ISBN: 978-1-4520-1681-8 (sc)
ISBN: 978-1-4520-1680-1 (hc)

PREFACE

Some people may think of this book as just another of those miserable heart wrenching stories, but each person's story is a true account of a precious life, which is real and unique, it's not just another abuse story. This is my story, which at the time was known only to the perpetrator and me. I could not possibly have known the outcome though I now know I did right in keeping my secret for so long.

I now pray it will help just one person in their healing process; and help them to realise they are not alone, and know they do not have to face their demons alone and to help people who have never uncounted such atrocities to understand that people do not make up stories like this.

God was there for me, in the torrents and turmoil of my life even when my life seemed hopeless, though at the time I thought he had given me up as lost. I still prayed my life would one day come good, when my life got back on track I would feel enabled to live a full life. I truly believed God was there for me, even during the depths of my pain and despair, and I know He can be there for you too; it's our choice which path we take. We can let our past control us or we can take control by being in charge of our own future and facing the past instead of hiding from it. Either way it is not easy, just when you feel you are seeing the light, another wave of doubt and disillusion sweeps over you. The memories will never go they cannot be erased but they do become less threatening, the pain eases and when you are healed it will be like a bad nightmare.

The word 'control' is used because abused people are usually under a controlling individual. I am now, with the help of God, in control of my own life, whereas in my past a man whom I should have loved and respected controlled me but instead there was hate and disregard, mixed up with wanting to be love, and approval which I'm told is a normal characteristic of abused people. If you are going through a time of abuse or healing from abuse you are not alone, it has happened to women and men throughout time immemorial and most abused victims go on to lead a "normal" life even with memories they cannot erase. If you can only do one thing in your life, you must forgive otherwise the hatred which lies beneath eats away at your soul destroying a beautiful person, which has been locked away for so many years.

Ask yourself why should another person go on ruining what is left of a life, only you can break the cycle.

INTRODUCTION

My Dad was the only boy in his family along with three sisters; his father was a seaman in the south of England. Much to his family's regret Dad joined the Army, this ruffled a few feathers, but Dad was a stubborn man. His father was both disappointed and angry. Dad was posted to Retford in Nottinghamshire, where I believe he stayed until the war ended. He never fought in the war although the stories he told us led us to believe he had.

Our grandparents on Dad's side of the family lived in Devon, in the south of England, where we often went for family holidays. My memory of Granddad was of a grumpy old man, sitting in the rocking chair next to a fireplace, chuffing on a pipe. He and Grandma lived in a lovely Victorian house with steps from the courtyard into a small garden, which led out to the tar pavement. When the weather was hot the tar melted. I remember my brother James and me poking sticks into the melted tar, tormenting each other running up and down the street. About 500 metres to the right of the tall wooden gate was a railway line we were not allowed to go up there for fear of getting squashed with a train, we did venture as close as we dare but if anyone found out we would have been for it big time.

The front door was made from beautiful coloured glass, blue, green and red. Through the door was a wide staircase with rooms either side; we liked to visit Granddad and Grandma's house, where Aunty Emily and her son Robert lived also. We loved to go for holidays, as they would take us for teddy hoggies on Coursands beach. The pasties were as big as half a dinner plate, hot and spicy, full of minced meat. We were never quite sure what the meat was, but it sure tasted good, mixed with lots of potato and bits of carrot and onion. We had some good times in Devon, James and I lived there for about four months when Robert our youngest brother was born prematurely, which led to him having feeding problems that continued throughout his childhood. Because Mam was also having problems with her health, James went to school in Plymouth for the four months we were there but I was too young at 4 years old, my memories are very vivid even at this young age. Aunty Emily would take me over the dunes to collect James from school picking blackberries to make homemade jam or pies. There were hundreds of wild flowers scattered all over the dunes. It was a beautiful site, as I lived with my family on a Nottingham housing estate.

I was always a happy fun loving child hopping and skipping and making others happy in my path; everyone loved me. Aunty Emily was always very kind to us and she treated us like her own children, at least whilst we lived under the same roof. Her son was much older than us and had his own friend's; his Dad was never seen by any of us we hadn't ever met him and we never questioned.

Granddad always went for a pint or two at 6 o'clock on the dot. He would be home for 7:30 and would fall asleep in his chair next to the fire with his mouth wide open snoring loudly. James and I were little monkeys and we would play tricks on him by putting our wax crayons into his mouth then we would run off. He used to go crazy and shout, "You bloody kids, wait till I get hold of you." Grandma would be furious and clip our ears then sent us to bed, but not before we all had a good giggle, and we could hear them laughing too, we never meant harm, it was such fun.

They did not have an indoor bath, for these were a real novelty in those days. The tin bath was kept on a nail outside the back door, which came into the kitchen once a week. Bath time was in front of the roaring fire, an experience to behold. Water was poured in via a huge steel jug, Grandma could hardly lift it, when it was considered to deep enough we would get in, and wash ourselves. We were not allowed to splash or else, we had been warned and generally obeyed our orders.

There was another tin bath outside sitting on bricks this one had rusty holes in it, James and I would fill it with cold water up to the holes. Aunty Emily would take us to a stream nearby to collect frogspawn and plants so we could create our very own pond in the back yard but grumpy Granddad seemed to moan about everything and he always told us off. He would shout "get rid of them bloody things, they will die anyway I don't want all those frogs hopping about the garden." Granddad often contradicted himself, and anyway they didn't die and a short time later tiny tadpole emerged which eventually turned into tiny frogs. I remember being amazed that the frogs came from what was to me a pile of slime. James and I would put them in a bucket and take them back to the stream minus the slime.

Most people called their Mother, Mum or Mummy, but for whatever reason our whole family called our Mother, Mam, our friends thought it a bit strange but she was our Mam. Mam was a gentle kind woman who would do anything for anyone, don't get me wrong she could bring a good wale mark in the shape of a hand to the skin on your bum or if she was off course it would be on the thigh should she need to demonstrate her anger, but in general she was a caring warm hearted Mam who really loved children and also enjoyed a good gossip with anyone who could spare 10 minutes. What Mam did not know about people who lived around us was not worth knowing, although I never knew her to be malicious or trouble causing she just liked to gossip.

Mam hardly ever wore makeup just a little lipstick on occasion, she never dressed herself with pride as the children always came first, her clothes were mainly A-line floral dresses which she made on the treadall sewing machine, the dresses did not have much style, but this was the 50s and 60s I'm talking about and I suppose anything went. Mam had a good thick head of hair, which looked presentable, it was auburn in colour and naturally wavy, but not much effort went into styling it, she would tie it back in a dark ribbon and hairgrips. I never knew her to own any luxury items like jewellery just her plain wedding ring, and the odd tin brooch, which she might pick up at a jumble sale; I do not remember her spending much money on herself at all.

My Mam was a Nottingham girl, with a family of 9 brothers and two sisters, a family born and bred in the small town of Bulwell, in Nottingham. Some of the family were in the building trade and some worked down the coalmines. They lived in a house not too far from 'the bogs', which is really the River Leen and still their today changed a little but in my eyes just the same. James and I spent many happy Saturday mornings fishing with a homemade fishing net made from an old net curtain and a beanpole. Mam, Dad or Aunt Bess would sew it all the way round to form a dip so we could catch our tiddlers, and a lot of floating weed with all sorts of life forms creeping around and wriggling inside it. We wore second hand black Wellie's on our feet, so we could paddle in the shallow parts of the river.

We tried hard not to let the water rise above our Wellie's but invariably it did and our socks squelched all the way home. We put everything we caught into empty jam jars, and then threw them back into the river, we were not allowed to take the tiny little fish home we did skive a few home but they always died.

Our Mam's Dad was always very nice to us, and he would treat us to a few coppers to spend on sweets, but Grandma was a bit mean and strict, not very patient with us at all though she did have a pretty hard life with 12 children in a three bed roomed Victorian house some of the children were all grown up and years between them so some had left home some were in the forces, but I guess at some point that house was heaving from the rafters can you imagine Christmas time when everyone got together and then some would have girlfriends and wives.

Grandma cleaned in the Grey friars pub to make ends meet so it was no wonder her patience was thin with another brood, I am sure she felt she had her share of children. My brother James and I had the task of dusting the dark wooden furniture. I always had the legs and cross bars of the huge wooden table to clean. Grandma would say "I am checking it when you've done." The table had a white table cloth that hung over all its sides, on the table there was always a large loaf of bread on a wooden board with a checked tea towel at the side, a butter dish with real butter in it, a jar of homemade jam, cups and saucers, a glass sugar bowl and a bottle of sterilised milk which I liked to drink though not in tea as it tasted horrid. Granddad was in charge of cutting the bread for the children he cut it very thin. James had to dust the huge wooden cabinet in the sitting room, which covered the entire wall; Granddad said it was full of all sorts of precious things including a bottle of sherry and a bottle of whiskey, which we never saw them drink but eventually the bottle did become empty.

In the room was a black Agar open fire with an oven to the side, which the cat would climb into to keep warm. I remember saying to Granddad the cat will cook and die Granddad, he would give a gentle smile and puff on his pipe and say cats are cleverer than you think, he knows where it's warm; he'll move when it gets too hot for him, don't you worry about that cat then he would smile and give a little chuckle under his breath. There was always a kettle or teapot bubbling away on the fire and sometimes a large pan of homemade soup with potatoes floating on the top. Granddad smoked a very shiny pipe and he would sit in a chair at the side of the fire with a tub of different coloured thin wood sticks, which he used to light his pipe. He would put the stick to the fire then to his pipe and puff, making the sound of a hungry fish. The smell would drift all over the room; it's funny how smells are remembered. There was a second tub with pipe cleaners which were long thin wiry things covered in a white fluffy cotton he used to poke down through to the other side of the pipe to clean it, his pipe was never very dirty as he was always giving it a good poke. He never really said a lot and I do not ever remember him getting cross with us kids, he was always very kind to us, and he smiled a lot but said very little.

We were only allowed to be in the back room, we were never allowed to go upstairs or in the front room where there was an aspidistra plant with great big leaves spreading across 3 feet and climbing 4 foot in height. It was in a huge brass bucket at the side of the grate. The house also had a scullery, which was freezing with a square pot sink in it and a wooden draining board with a mangle on top of a tub. This sat on a quarry-tiled floor; which was very cold on our feet because we all had to take our shoes off at the back door. There was a cooker under the stairs, though I never saw it being used. Each Saturday morning we all gathered here at our Grandparents house;

the adults would drink tea and gossip about what was happening to those who were absent from the gathering.

Mam had joined the NAAFI and was posted to Retford. That's where Mam and Dad met until they eventually married in 1944. A year and a bit later Mam gave birth to George my eldest brother, followed by John, James, me, Robert, June and finally Carol, seven children in total. They lived in a terraced house in Carlton but later moved into a one-year-old house on a nice estate the other side of town, in Aspley.

Mam was expecting me at the time they moved in. I was born in the front room at about 3am on Wednesday May 12th, 1954 and I was the first girl after three boys to join the family. Mam was very happy. The neighbours and midwife all mucked in to deliver me, not too much trouble apparently, a fairly easy birth. After 3 boys she was pleased to have a girl, which outweighed any pain I had caused during childbirth.

Dad worked down various coalmines most of his married life, and Mam did a night shift at the City Hospital as an orderly. She made tea for the patients and did any night cleaning if patients had vomited or needed their bed sheets changing. She worked hard between the night shifts then coming home to sort our lot out, all our bed sheets had 'hospital property' embroidered in the top corner, but they were nice clean white crisp cotton sheets so we never asked any questions. Dad also worked shifts so there was usually someone at home with us to look after the children. They were mostly happy times; money was tight but Dad grew all sorts of vegetables in a modestly sized garden, which helped keep a meal on the table.

George and Dad would go shooting for wood pigeons and wild rabbits down the viaducts with our Alsatian dog that ran to collect the game. Dad would spend time plucking or skinning whatever they brought home and we would have a game pie, with loads of spuds/potatoes and cabbage for supper, which I have to say, was yummy. Dad was the cook in our house; he was a good cook and a good Dad at that time.

The local church jumble sale and the wishing book (a catalogue where goods are ordered and paid for weekly) kept us all in clothes and shoes. It was not always what we wanted but we were mostly fully clothed and had to be grateful. Also Mam was very clever at the sewing machine and with the knitting needles so between the ideals we were not too badly off. We always had warm jumpers and cardigans to wear. I remember she even knitted socks, mittens, hats, scarves and not forgetting the cot blankets, which I soon learnt to knit myself, as there always seemed to be a baby in the house.

The change began sometime between 1963 and 1965 though for what reason I will never know. Nothing happened out of the ordinary to my knowledge, with the exception of the miners' strike, which had no bearing on me, as I was just a little girl. I have to admit Mam always seemed pregnant to me and when she was not pregnant she was ill. I know she had terrible times with her periods. I remember there being blood all over the sheets and often on the clothes she was wearing. She always had a great big pad between her legs and if she could not afford to buy towels she would use pieces of ripped up sheet which she would leave to soak in a bucket then wash and dry them ready to be reused next time. I feared having the same ordeal but I knew nothing of women's periods, as it was never explained to me until it actually happened. I dreaded the thought of me having to wear rags between my legs; of bleeding from my private area and so I decided it only happened to older women. I asked Mam, but she said when you are a women you will find out, so my theory seemed right at the time.

Robert was born after me in 1958, then came June in 1961 and soon after Carol was born in December 1962. I know the doctor said that Mam was not to have any more kids/children after she had Robert, who was always under weight and often visiting the hospital, but Dad being Dad did not agree, and although he was not a Catholic or any religion for that matter, he did not agree to using contraception. I think he saw women as breeding machines and as far as he was concerned, a woman was put on the earth for man's desire and to bear children and to clean and cook. Soon after Carol was born Mam took quite ill and had to have a hysterectomy because cancer cells were present. I am grateful for my sisters but Mam could have done without any more kids, because she just got sicker and sicker. By the time Carol, who was the 7th Child was born, Mam was tired and in a lot of pain, which was not the fault of the kids she bore, it was the fault of Dad being so ignorant. Mam was only 39 years old when she was diagnosed with the cancer, and her pain and suffering lasted for five years until she died at the age of 44.

CHAPTER ONE

THE BIRTH OF A DAUGHTER

I was born on the 12th May 1954 In Nottingham Dad was walking home from his night shift at work when one of the neighbours came out and told him he had a daughter. Dad cried when he first saw me, his first-born daughter. He was elated and he celebrated for days with both family and friends, it was said he loved the very skin I was in. I had three brothers older than me and one brother and two sisters, who were to be born later. Through the years we had dogs, cats and later a few chickens and rabbits, even a couple of ducks at one time. We lived in a three bedroom council house; a middle house of three with an average sized back garden. There was a shed at the back, a small-grassed area and vegetables for all seasons down one side. In the front garden there was a grassed area, rose trees and a hedge all the way around the perimeter. The house was in a reasonably good area, with nice people around us, and we were happy most of the time whilst I was young whilst I do not remember anything before I was four years old but I believe times were good. However, life can be cruel and unpredictable as the years passed on my life was dealt with cruel times right there in the house where I was born.

Mam had two sisters Bessie and Doris who we called Aunt Bess and Aunt Dot. They were very good to Mam; in fact they were very good to all of us. They had no children of their own. They had no reason why they never had children; it was not pursued in those days. So the fault, if it could be called a fault, lay with no one, the aunties would say it was God's will that they had no children themselves, because Mam had so many, more than enough for all of them. It was good for us that the aunties didn't have any children because Mam desperately needed their help when she got very ill. The aunties didn't like our Dad for reasons of their own. He was an arrogant and bombastic man, so it was not surprising really, but they were there for Mam financially and very supportive in her hour of need. As much as I loved them however I could not confide in them for fear of the consequences, so I felt they were not there for me although I loved them very much. They were there in one sense but not there if you know what I mean but this will become clearer as you read on. I really felt that they should have known my unhappiness just by knowing me all my life, but no, this was to be my secret because I hadn't to tell a soul. My life would carry these secrets until it was time to reveal them and at that time revelation was not possible. Not even my lovely aunties could help, as they could not see my pain. They never suspected anything was wrong with me; they knew Mam had the odd bruise and told her to leave him. Though they didn't like Dad and felt sorry for Mam being married to him, they never knew just how bad her life was but what could they have done? There were seven children to consider and who would want to take care of seven children if they were to interfere in the marriage and the parents split up they would not have been thanked for it and people in those days just got on with it and said God gave them their lot and that was that there were not the choices we have today.

I had prayed to Jesus for as long as I could remember and although Mam and Dad hardly ever went to church they encouraged James and I to go. None of the others went, with the exception of midnight mass on Christmas Eve, or a special occasion. The Midnight Mass Service began at around 11.15. We would get our warm coats off our beds which had doubled up as blankets and walk down to the Christ Church, passing the closed shops and the dark wood yard on the right, which was pretty scary at night with big giant motors and chains dangling from high. It would take us the best part of 20 minutes. Dad would meet us outside the church after the pubs had shut, well on his way to being drunk, he would end up snoring and farting in his pew, whilst we all sang carols by candlelight, with the giant Christmas tree glistening with pretty lights which draped down. The tree stood proud at the front of church next to the pulpit, where the vicar stood to give his sermon. A choir sat in rows at the front of the church facing each other; they all wore long gowns, which flowed, to the hard stone floor. It was accepted that men on the back row were drunk so Dad was not the only drunk man there; it was commonplace. Midnight Mass was fun and different and I liked it.

I am a big believer in family closeness and being altogether in church was somehow a special moment for me. Maybe that's why the memory is so strong, I felt a sense of belonging to God, whom I believed in with all my heart and Jesus who would be my friend throughout my life, although I did not see it at the time. Sometimes I felt closer to God than other times; sometimes he seemed a million miles away. Whilst I never doubted God, at times he just was not there for me, and I felt abandoned by Him, alone in my own tormented misery.

James and I sometimes played 'Happy Home'; we played it in the garden using the garden shed as our home. I fetched a tea set from my toy box and James fetched his red pedal car, which he could sit in, and pedal; it was a bit battered but still resembled a car. We had some fun on these occasions and would swap roles sometimes but we were young and things had not changed yet within our real family. We were in a happy home with lots of laughter and food was plentiful, so I do not know why James and I called this game 'Happy Home'.

I made us dinner from mud and leaves and flowers, a few worms and nice crunchy snails all from Dad's garden. Dad said that you could eat the orange flower petals, which were called Nasturtiums, as they were edible. We did try them but it did not seem right even though we saw Dad eat one and I remember he also ate a Daffodil petal but we didn't. Dad also let bumble bees walk on his hands and said a bee will never hurt unless it feels threatened.

There were lots of garden tools in the shed and a single bed but I didn't know why that was in there until much later in life, when I heard it was a 'love bed' for George and his girlfriends, or an escape for him when he was falling out with Dad. There was a long window with a dirty greyish coloured net curtain across it on a wire preventing anyone looking in or out and Dad had rigged a light up. For a time it was fun playing 'Happy Homes'. Mam let us have jam sandwiches and some squash and some broken biscuits so we played out there for hours. Sometimes friends joined us but often we were just on our own having fun laughing and generally chatting and playing make believe.

Why did it have to stop, we were so happy, so very happy. Why does life have to change so dramatically, to cause so much misery? Mam once said life never stays still, time and people move on. I wanted my life as a 5/6 year old to last forever, when James and I were best friends and no one else mattered. Mam and Dad seemed happy then too, but the babies kept coming, along with the hardships and arguments, which seemed to come with them.

CHAPTER TWO

EASTER PARADE

At Easter the whole family would attend church again, this time Dad went to the pub after church. Dad would cook the whole dinner very early on Easter morning so it could be finished off or warmed up and ready to dish up when we got home. Dad could make a meal out of virtually nothing and so can I even today. Dad taught me how to cook and let me carve the meat or turkey at Christmas and Easter. Mam was not very good in the kitchen the food was either under cooked or burnt, in fact when I was tall enough to reach the kitchen worktop I did the cooking whilst Dad was at work. I started cooking and cleaning when I was about eight years old.

At the Easter service Mam would parade us in our new outfits, which Mam would either knit, or buy from the wishing book, on a weekly account. My dress was always lovely with a huge bow tied to the back; I always had a bonnet usually straw with chicks or flowers stuck to the side, which I wore with pride. Although I liked hats, I would fidget with it and want to wear it how I wanted, not as it should be worn. June and Carol were always dressed in identical dresses, which were always very pretty with lots of bows and ribbons and with homemade cardigans to match, white socks and new shoes. The congregation would comment "Look at those dear children don't they look smart, she does very well with so many mouths to feed." Mam was very proud at the sympathetic comments that were made and gossiped to one or two of them in the pews.

My memories of the hymns we sang depended on what time of year it was, I particularly liked, What a Friend We Have in Jesus, it went like this.

What a friend we have in Jesus, all our sins and grief's to bear!
What a privilege to carry everything to God in prayer!
O what peace we have to forfeit, O what needless pain we bear – all because we do not carry everything to God in prayer!

And I did pray, every night without fail. I was not forced or encouraged to pray, it was my choice. I had very few choices but no one could take away my choice to pray, after all it was my refuge. This was my silent prayer, which no one could touch, not even Dad and possibly it was the only thing that kept me sane throughout my ordeal.

My brother James would take me into Sunday school, on an ordinary Sunday. When we went, we walked hand in hand. People who did not know us always thought we were twins; in fact we were a little like twins with only ten and a half months between us. But then as we got older I stopped going to church because of James. He would hit me on the way and his friends would call me names and make me cry. His reputation was at stake; it's not the done thing having your kid sister tagging along. He then joined a different church, St Leo's Church at Basford, Nottingham. James had a beautiful voice and sang in the choir. He, along with the other boys and men all wore a robe which was white with a red collar, and if you looked closely you could see which boys had dirty shoes under the long robes. Then his voice broke and he stopped singing in the choir. In fact he stopped going to church altogether; he claimed he was an atheist and that he only joined the choir to please Mam. I knew the real reason he stopped believing. It was hard to believe in God when you had a Dad who beat you regularly. Although our parents said they loved us, it was hard to comprehend the Jekyll and Hyde behaviour that began to emerge. Sometimes it felt like we children went unnoticed because our parents were too wrapped up worrying about money or where the next meal was coming from or even how they would be able to afford to buy our clothes.

I believed it was partly my fault James got a beating on a regular basis or at least I thought it was at the time. I would snitch to Dad about something James had done or someone else that James had hit me or he'd done this or that tittle-tattle to get him in trouble. Sometimes he was just caught in the act giving me a thump or hitting the young ones. Mostly he hit out over very trivial things and sometimes there was no reason at all. Only James knew why he lashed out all the time but I was the only one who understood his pain. The beatings he took from Dad were very harsh. He would curl up in the corner of the front room whilst Dad hit him with a stick, he hit and hit, and I felt his pain. We had a nickname for the stick Dad used to beat James with, it was the poky stick, made of some sort of fibrous wood greyish in colour and was about 12 inches long and about 1 inch in diameter. It was a very old stick and Mam used it to poke the washing down into the dolly tub on washdays. The poky stick would become James' nightmare. Dad would hit him and carry on hitting him until James apologised. Even after his apology Dad would say, "These are for luck." Dad would shout, "Don't hit the young ones again" but James continued hitting us for reasons I didn't understand.

I would shout for Dad to stop beating him, and Dad shouted, "It's the only way for him to learn, he needs to know he cannot go around hitting you young ones." I suppose there was logic in there somewhere, where Dad was concerned, but it did not make sense to me. Dad would say "I will teach you a lesson you little bastard" stop him hitting your brothers and sisters then proceeded to knock the living daylights out of him, by beating him senseless. Dad would shout "Marie get out." So many times I stood crying in the hallway, saying I was sorry to James until Dad shouted even louder, "Will you go away." I hated it, and hated Dad for doing it, but it never stopped Dad hitting James or James hitting me. Dad did stop beating him eventually but not until James was sobbing with the pain he endured. I honestly believe Dad got some sort of perverse pleasure watching him cry in pain. I cried myself to sleep many a night knowing I had caused my brother, whom I loved so much, that kind of pain. I prayed to Jesus, if only James could just be good to us, then he would not get a beating, but then it all would go around again, one vicious circle.

When we were children, the arguments, which happened, were not measured by the misery that was created. At the time the measurement was who could score the most points by snitching to our Mam or Dad. We did not know what we were doing or I am sure we would not have told on each other. There was no doubt Dad was a bully. It was always said I was the favourite, mainly because I was the first-born girl. Everyone called me Daddy's little girl; even Mam was cruel at times. She also called me "Daddy's favourite girl". I have to wonder why she would say "Go to Daddy, Daddy's favourite child, Daddy's favourite girl." She must have agreed to what went on behind the closed doors, or did she? Maybe only I knew.

I had learnt the Lord's Prayer off by heart. It was the only thing that the Sunday school had requested from all the children. They said it was a good basis for prayer, and if everyone would say it and mean it each day, they would not go far wrong. In fact the best way to live your life was through the Lord's Prayer. They used to say think about the words, when you pray them and I did just that, I would alter the words a little to suit me.

My father in heaven, great is thy name.

Thy Kingdom come, thy will be done, on earth as it is in heaven.

Give me this day and my daily bread.

Forgive me my trespasses as I try to forgive those who trespass against me.

Lead me not into temptation, but deliver me from evil.

For thine is the kingdom, the power and the glory, for ever and ever Amen.

Every night as I lay in bed I would say the Lord's Prayer followed by "And Lord Jesus, bless Mam, Dad, James and the rest of my brothers and sisters and anyone else who knows me." This prayer was prayed for many years to come, even if I had been beaten or abused that day, my trespasses still got blessed, no matter what, I knew it was the right thing for me to do.

CHAPTER THREE

CHRISTMAS 1962

As Christmas approached in 1962 I started to pray for something else after my prayer of blessing for my family: a dolls house. I never thought of anything else. I told my brother John how I had always dreamt of having my very own dolls house. He said "Well you never know you might get one." He was very good to me and encouraged me in my schoolwork and showed me how to memorise the times table. I had some difficult homework where I had to do research and he introduced me to the library and I got an "A" for that particular assignment which was about volcanoes.

The dolls house in the catalogue was made from plastic, in a beige colour with a brown roof and holes for the windows and doors; it was nice but not quite the same as the one on Blue Peter, which was made of wood. That one looked like a real house, with shutters on the outside of the windows, a door, which opened, and a chimney pot protruding out of the roof. Lovely flowers were painted on the outside walls.

I watched Blue Peter every week, and they were making a dolls house. One week they made a pond out of cooking foil, trees out of pipe cleaners and cotton wool. Of course Blue Peter had dressed their house and put curtains at all the windows. Every week they showed how to make different things for it until it was complete. I loved it; I was looking forward to transforming a plain wood house into a special dolls house, which I would create. I was making mental notes in my head of everything they did week by week. I did not mind what it was made from, as long as I got one. I had already started to make my tiny pieces of furniture out of Dad's empty matchboxes and burnt off matches, bottle tops and bobbins. In fact I collected anything that I thought I could cover with paper or fabric to make a piece of furniture for the dolls house. I kept everything until I had enough bits to make more furniture; I could make almost any piece of furniture out of the simplest bit of tat. I kept all my bits and bobs in a shoebox under my bed, which I shared with my sister June, and brother Robert. They were both very young but knew not to touch the box. Whilst I shared my things, this was out of bounds; I would get the beautiful dolls house for Christmas, and would have my homemade furniture to go inside. It was promised from Santa, I was convinced that he said I would receive one for Christmas, and after all he did ask me what I had wanted. Auntie Bess had taken James and me to see Santa; James was only 10 ½ months older than me. I sat on Santa's knee even though I was a little old for that sort of thing. We believed in Santa for longer in those days, and it was always said if you don't believe in Santa you don't get gifts so we just did as we were told.

I wrote a letter to Santa, though goodness knows where it was sent. It was just in case he had misheard me or worse still, not heard at all, as he was very old with his white beard and big tummy, and all dressed in red and white, with green faced elves at his side. I said I wanted one thing in the whole world, I remember he said "Now what can it be?" I replied "A dolls house." Santa even asked me how many bedrooms I would like the house to have. I was quite precise and said four bedrooms would be fine as it was for a big family and it must have a bathroom, the same as the one on Blue Peter. I told him knowing that he would know the exact one I meant as Santa was magical, and all knowing, and he knew all about us, just as the vicar did at the church since he said God knew every single hair on our head. Santa knew how important it was for me and asked me if I would like anything else, I answered "No, but may I ask a question?"

Santa nodded and said "Yes, ask anything you want." I asked him the question, "Does Santa take toys back once they have been given on Christmas Day?" I saw Santa look at Aunt Bess and he said

"No, not usually." I interrupted him saying "Not even if I have been naughty?" Santa said "No, Santa would never take the toys off little children; your Mam might not let you play with them for a while if you are naughty, but he would never take them back." When Aunt Bess was out of earshot of Santa, she asked me what I meant but I could not tell her as I did not know how to, all I knew is that my toys always disappeared shortly after Christmas. Aunt Bess mumbled that it was a strange question to ask and my brother James never clicked on to what I was talking about, but later it would make sense to both of us. I was a little confused but happy with the answer and we all let it go at that.

I told all my friends I was having a dolls house for Christmas. It was a big thing to ask for, so they laughed at me and said there are too many kids in your family so bet you don't get one. When I asked why, one of them said well Santa only has so much money to spend and if your family all had big gifts, we would not get any so that's why you get small gifts like colouring books and crayons. My friends, if that's what you call them, were laughing at me, taunting and poking fun at my belief. They said Santa is a story, he's not real, stupid, and yer Mam buys yer the gifts, not Santa. Yer must be really stupid if yer still believe in Santa. I was upset at the remark but said that I liked colouring books and crayons there is nothing wrong with them. I don't believe in Santa really it's just the young ones who believe, but we all have to pretend in our house. Then another girl shouted "Bet you get socks and knickers and things like that too, not toys like normal children, we get proper gifts and toys." I knew they were being cruel at the time, but they were right, I did get socks and knickers. They always got really nice things and wore nice clothes and I never saw them at the jumble sales we went to. They wore real shoes, whereas I wore Wellies or plastic jellybean shoes. I always had a new pair of shoes from the coupon shop for Easter, but I never saw any of my so called friends in the coupon shop where we went. They did not queue for free dinners at school either. We even paid with coupons not money for our uniforms and sometimes we got a treat if there was enough.

I never knew until years later, when Mam said it was an allowance for big families. We did not question why in those days, and our parents did not think we needed to know. If you didn't know you could not talk about it. What my so called friends said did make sense, and as we were one of the biggest families in the area, it was a wonder Santa came to us at all, but I was adamant I was getting a dolls house.

Chapter Four

Jack Frost

Christmas Day arrived, I had been awake very early, and I just lay there. There was no sound coming from the rest of the house.

I knew not to go downstairs without the others, as it was still dark outside. I looked out of the small rectangle windows, which were frozen with ice on both sides of the glass. I scratched faces of snowmen, stars, and angels in the ice, and made a wish to Jack Frost which was an imaginary figure in one's mind some feared him some made wishes to him it was always said it was a him I suppose because his name was Jack though where he came from I don't know but Mam used to say if you are out after dark on Winters night Jack Frost would get you, and if it was after 10.00 pm she would say the 10 o'clock horses would get you it was quite frightening to a child all these old wives tales.

The ice fell like snow onto the windowsill and eventually thawed out into small puddles of water as I breathed over it. It was still and very cold outside. There was a grey fur animal, which was our cat curled up into a ball on some of the rabbit's straw in the coalbunker just below my window. No one had called him in last night. He liked to be out all night but no one realised just how cold it was going to be that night.

The plants in the garden looked stiff, white and lifeless and yet beautiful, they looked as though someone had sprinkled them with glitter like that on the Christmas cards. I could just see some tiny footprints on the iced path leading up the garden to the shed maybe tiny mice or birds made them. The shed resembled Santa's grotto, which James and I decorated just two weeks earlier. Everywhere was almost as still as a picture in a frame. The wood holding the glass in place resembled the picture frame as I peeped through the hole where I had scratched in the ice, and strained to see anything that was different after all it was Christmas morning.

Mam had helped to put paper chains across the ceiling in our bedroom so it was all Christmassy, all brightly coloured and pretty, Mam and I always changed the sheets one week before Christmas so the bedroom was all clean for when the Aunties came, not that they came upstairs, only to use the toilet. I was still daydreaming when I heard Dad get up. I knew it was nearly time, to go downstairs, I was bursting inside with excitement and I was thanking God for what I might receive by way of a dolls house. I waited in my room patiently; I lifted a box from the wardrobe, which held all my pieces of handmade furniture. I checked each piece was intact then in my mind I placed it into the rooms of the house. Lost in my dream, I heard Carol crying. Now Mam would have to wake, but I knew she would not go downstairs until the fire was lit. Carol stopped crying and I heard Mam shuffling around which indicated Mam had laid Carol in her bed, for a little while, until the lounge was warmed up. All was quiet with the exception of Dad cleaning out the grate of the coal fire.

Mam said we were moving into the big bedroom after Christmas because baby Carol was now big enough to come in with us. She informed us there would be a set of bunk beds, a single bed and a cot for baby Carol. I asked what bunk beds were and she said, "You'll see soon enough, they are fun and you can choose which one you want to sleep in." I remember thinking that might not be much fun, with the young uns crying half the night. I did love Carol but I already had June and Robert, and James was coming in with us as well which I was excited about but I knew he did not like noise and I knew we would have problems with the babies or rather I would have the problems. It's hard to keep babies quiet and I would surely have that job. All this was so George could have his own room because he was now paying Mam board and wanted some space. He would share it with John when he was home on leave from the navy, so indirectly he had his own room whilst four of us shared.

When Mam went downstairs with baby Carol, it was then I knew the fire would be backed up. I had heard Dad rattling the grate and carrying buckets from the back door in to the lounge. We had four large buckets in the kitchen so the coal was dry enough to light the fire.

I waited a little while longer and then went down. I was so excited about finding my dolls house that I simply did not want to wait for the others, but knew I had to. I just wanted to get downstairs. I was shivering with cold, so I put on my pink dressing gown that was a little too small, as it was from Santa two years ago. Mam said I had had a growing spurt, but it was still warm when I buttoned up the front. I drew the thin cotton curtains back and it had started to snow, which made Christmas Day all the more special. I always liked the snow. We had such fun because there were a lot of us and we would team up with other families on the road. It was something we could all join in with; mind you I nearly always got bombarded with icy snowballs from my brothers. They would inevitably make me cry at some stage of the game because they were so rough and it hardened me up from the sweet little girl into a bit of a tomboy but still I liked being a girl and loved girlie things.

I enjoyed putting on pretty dresses and dressing up in Mam's shoes. Although Mam did not wear much make up she always had a lipstick or two and she did not mind me using it. She said how pretty I looked, but I felt plain and uninteresting, unlike my best friend who had long blond hair and a milky white skin. Her Mam dressed her in really nice dresses, which had been bought from a shop. I have to admit I was a little envious of her way of life because she had dancing and piano lessons. I used to spend a lot of time at her house, when I was not helping with the babies. Linda had her own hairbrush in her own drawer and one of her chores was to tidy the drawer and clean the hair out of the brush. If that was my only chore, if only I had a hairbrush of my own I thought. She had a tin in the drawer with a mixture of sweets and chocolate bars; she had them as an allowance. They called it a tuck box and sometimes she shared one with me.

I envied her life a little but she also envied mine. She was sometimes lonely and had to practice on the piano every evening. I can honestly say my life wasn't dull or lonely. Linda did have a sister, so I could not understand Linda being lonely, but we got on great, and I could escape for an hour without babies attached to my hip.

I knew Santa had been because there hooked to the bottom of the bed were three stockings full of nice things to eat. I was not interested in my stocking; I needed to look for my dolls house. Robert was only 4 years old and he had woken up. I knelt and looked out of the window again with Robert, I liked to look out the window. I used to daydream to the stars at night, whilst the others were in bed early and I had to stay with them until they fell asleep. Then I could go downstairs for half an hour before my bedtime. Robert still wore a nappy at night and he smelt really strongly of wee (Urine) as he stood up beside me. He asked if Santa had been, in a sleepy tone, half smiling at the snow falling. I said, "Yes, but the presents will be under the tree downstairs." His pyjamas were wet down the inside of his leg, so it delayed getting to the Christmas presents, as I had to take off his wet clothes. I laid him down to take his nappy off, pulled down the rubber pants, which held the nappy in place and was also supposed to stop the sides leaking but hardly ever worked the wee just leaked out. I undid the large safety pin and lifted his bottom up to remove the nappy. "There you go," I said "Use the potty like a big boy now." I put him some clean pyjamas on and his dressing gown, "There, are you nice and warm?" He smiled and said "All right Marie"; Robert was a happy little boy. Always underweight he had trouble as a baby keeping his food down, but turned out all right in the end. He always got treats like cakes and sweets, because Mam said he needed fattening up. Dad would say that about the chickens which he kept in the back garden, so connecting the two was funny really as we all knew the chickens would end up on the table one day surrounded with spuds and other vegetables.

June woke up. She was only fourteen months. She was a pretty baby and had big brown eyes and chubby rosy cheeks. We nicknamed her 'hammy', as it looked like she had stored her food in her cheeks. She wriggled and cried then kicked the covers off and flung her arms in the air, as if we were going to leave her. I knew that could never happen as she was always attached to my hip, wherever I went June was with me. The neighbours said you will suffer with that hip my girl when you get older. I would laugh and say we were Siamese twins never to be separated they would say cheeky madam, and sure enough that hip has had to be replaced at the age of 54, I have to say those

Neighbours were right about having worn out joints.

June's nappy stank and was loaded as well so I lifted her up and said "Poo smelly" and she giggled. I took off her baby-grow then the rubber pants, and the nappy, which was really dirty, I cleaned her the best I could. I asked Robert to go get some toilet roll, which we had because it was Christmas. It might be newspaper on string next week. I wiped her but the brown mess was like glue stuck to her bum, she was very sore as she was full of a bad cold. She cried, so I said "Poo stinky bum, stinky bum trying to make light of it." Then she giggled and stopped crying, I got as much as I could off with the dry hard toilet roll then just left it, as I knew she would be bathed soon, I fastened her baby-grow up and put on her a cardigan. She already had socks on because we all went to bed in our socks to keep our feet warm.

We all loved Christmas and the snow was nice but the house felt very cold. Robert was excited and was telling June about Christmas to keep her happy. He bundled the stocking in front of her, she did not have a clue why or what it was really. I said "Be careful with the sweet wrappers, put the stuff back in the stocking it will be warmer when we go downstairs." I wanted them to wait because I had been awake and seemed to be waiting ages and I did not care about what was in the stockings really. I just wanted to get down the stairs. They did as I asked and pushed the goodies back into the red felt stocking, which Mam had made on her sewing machine. Robert said, "Come on June there are more presents from Santa downstairs aren't there Marie?" I answered "Yes, let's go" and Robert passed me my stocking. "Aren't you going to just look what's inside yours Marie?" I replied, "When I get downstairs I will." I knew what was in it, because it was the same every year. We jumped off the double bed, which all three of us slept in, although the room was very cold.

When snuggled in we all soon got warm, unless one of them wet through their nappy onto the bed, then I would feel a warm trickle down my back as June slept one side and Robert slept the other. We had coats on top of the blankets for extra warmth. There was a wardrobe against the wall behind the door, which was full of clothes for all ages, and very untidy. I was warned not to open the wardrobe when the aunties came. We were happy, in our own way, and my happiness was bubbling over today.

Robert was eating a sweet he found in his stocking when he shouted to me in a muffled voice because the toffee was too big to eat and speak as well, "Don't forget your stocking." I rushed back with June on my hip, I picked up my stocking and was then handed two more, as Robert could not get down the stairs with them in his hand. We were all on the landing, when James burst open the door of his room. It swung back and crashed against the wall, he shared the room with George and John when he was home. This was the room we were due to move into. It had a fire grate in the corner which would be lit on the days we had plenty of coal so that room was warm, George never wanted to get out of bed, though the warmth of the fire did not stop ice forming up on the window panes. They looked marbled and white with lines and sparkly patterns on them. The room had no carpet on the floor, although there was a strip of frayed matting at the side of the two single beds and a wardrobe on the other wall. There was a set of drawers, and a cupboard over the stairs, which also had hanging space in it, but usually was full of clothes just thrown in, which was great when playing hide and seek.

George was bellowing very loudly "Get back to bed it's too early." He was too old to enjoy Christmas morning as he was more into the nightlife over Christmas than the gifts and Santa, I am sure we all shouted together, "It's Christmas George."

James slammed the door shut but it opened again. We thought we were going to get a good hiding, but he just wanted the toilet, and muttered, "I know it's Christmas but some of us are trying to sleep." We were giggling with excitement, except for June who was whing-ing; she did whinge a lot. She was still wondering what was going off so I put my fingers to my lips and tried to hush everyone, "Be quiet till you get downstairs," I said. I stumbled downstairs with two wet nappies in one hand and June attached to my hip, I passed the stockings to James and he held Robert's hand. We entered the lounge to music on the television, a service from a cathedral and a choir singing Silent Night, Holy Night all is calm all is bright. I stood and listened interested and affected by the whole Christmas thing. I was in my element. I loved Christmas and Silent Night has always reduced me to tears. I have no idea why because I cannot reach that particular memory.

Mam was washing baby Carol in front of the fire, which was now blazing up the chimney and extremely hot if you got too close. I had the nappies in my hand, Mam said "Take them into the kitchen and put them in a bucket, Dad's in there." In those days nappies were made of towelling, and had to be soaked in cold water to dilute the wee Mam said, then it stopped them becoming yellow. Carol slept in Mam's room in a crib. I think Mam was hoping for a Christmas baby as her birthday was on Christmas Eve, but Carol came early on the 5th December. Mam had a hard time, or so I heard Dad say, but after six previous children it was hardly surprising.

Over in the corner, June sat on the floor emptying her Santa stocking, with Robert's help. In the stockings were a blood orange, a little red apple, a sweet chewy bar, a sherbet dab, a few sweets at the bottom and a new knitted hat and mittens. They varied in colour and shape according to age, but we all had pretty much the same in our stockings. George and John had a bar of chocolate in theirs and an onion and a potato in there just for fun. June began crying because she did not understand what the fuss was about and she had a bad cold, which did not help. Her little nose was very red and sore. I asked Robert to watch her, as I knew Mam would need my help. Robert was good to her and helped to undo her gifts, as Mam was too busy with Carol. June had her nose pushed out when Carol was born just as James did when I was born. It's just one of those things with big families. Mam did not have the time for us all, but always tried her best. June was not sure what was happening with the new baby and clung to me more than ever when Carol was born. She would say "Marie." I lifted her up and I took her to Mam so she could bathe her in the old yellow plastic bath, which was looking past its date. It had been passed down from one child to another. I am not sure how old it was, but it could have been mine. It was placed on a table in front of the fire; Mam handed Carol to me and said, "Put her in her carry cot." She was dressed in a pretty red velvet dress with white frilly pants and red bows on, which went over her nappy; on her tiny little feet were white lacy socks, and a white cardigan with red rose buds on which Mam had knitted. She looked like a little doll and at only 3 weeks old, she was the size of a doll. In fact I had one bigger than her.

Carol was very pale looking, with a milky white skin, blue eyes and blond hair. She had an almost angelic look about her; she looked beautiful. June would be dressed identically after she was bathed. I told Mam she had messed in her nappy and it was really smelly. Mam smiled and said, "Not for long", and rubbed her nose against June's very pink nose. Her cheeks were big and rosy and very sore due to her having a cold; June had big brown eyes and brown hair she was a very loving cuddly child and she clung to me like I was her Mam. Whereas Carol was the opposite and did not really like being hugged, mind you she was only 3 weeks old but she did not like too much hugging throughout her childhood. Carol was clean, warm and content in her pretty outfit, which was a red velvet dress, white cardigan and bib, and tiny white socks. I gave Carol her bottle propped up on a folded blanket, Mam had taught me what to do, and it came naturally without instruction, she said, "Just be careful you don't drop her."

We would normally get dressed on the landing, or downstairs. The wooden floorboards were so cold in the bedrooms, so we would all run downstairs to huddle in front of the roaring fire. At least there was lino on the lounge floor, though it was freezing cold to touch, it stopped the drafts. In front of the fire was a brown half moon rug, which snuggled up to the hearth. It had hard crusty black coal burns all over it, which were made by the cinders when the fire was being transferred from one room to another in metal buckets, and bits of coal jumped out of the grate and landed onto the carpet and thankfully fizzled out. The carpet had its own story to tell, but anything was better to the toes than cold lino. The room had a small real Christmas tree in front of the back window. Tinsel and baubles in every colour you could think of covered the tree with lots of home-made sparkly designs; an angel took pride of place sitting on the top. Pretty lights would flash on and off in a system on their own. There were garlands of paper chains, which all linked into the centre light, which was a wooden three light chandelier and shiny shapes cascaded in between each triangle, it looked amazing. Christmas cards covered both windowsills and the fire mantel and wherever there was a shelf there was a card, and a long rope of cards led from one wall to another right across the mirror.

We had a sofa, two chairs, a cabinet, with glass doors, stood in the corner which housed glasses, decanters and jugs of all shapes and sizes and nice ornaments, none of us children was allowed to go in it just in case something got broken, the curtains had shapes of brown intermingled with orange and green, but they were very thin and old. Above the mantel was a picture of a scene from a farm; it had a man with a horse drawn plough in the middle of a large field there was lots of autumn trees and a river running through it. We used to play spot the fisherman but we could never find him, because he was not really in the picture. It was fun looking and sometimes we could imagine him there, and we really believe it, on the Opposite wall was a large mirror with hand painted red roses around the outside it had wavy corners and hung on a chain.

The light from the flames of the coal fire would sometimes catch something shiny. The reflection would glisten on the walls and move all around the room. Mam called it Johnny Noddy, it amused us for hours, we didn't always know what caused the small glimmer of light but sometimes it was Mam's watch. She would direct her watch towards the flames in the fire and move her wrist so the reflection moved around the walls and ceiling. We would run around the room trying to catch Johnny Noddy and try to guess where it was coming from.

Dad nearly always made a fire first thing in the morning for the family to get up to, a pan of porridge would be bubbling on the stove in the kitchen but not this particular morning. Although Dad was in the kitchen, he was seeing to the huge turkey. The stuffing mix was home made using bread, sage, an onion and an apple. Dad stuffed the turkey until it squelched out the other side of the bird. He said "Marie this is to keep the bird nice and moist; you should be helping Daddy really." I remember saying I would like that but I was helping Mam. Dad knew I loved to cook. The turkey was a bonus gift from the coal board; it was so big it could only just fit in the oven. There were saucepans full of potatoes, sprouts and carrots. Mushy peas were soaking in a bowl of water, which contained a soda tablet. All this food was prepared Christmas Eve. There were lots of chopped onions in another pan for the onion sauce and bread-crumbs on a plate for the bread sauce, there was also a large plate of homemade mince pies, which I helped to make, but Dad was the cook in our house. Mam always cooked mid week dinner, as Dad was at work but the meals she cooked were not a patch on Dad's. He baked bread; fruitcakes and he made his own pastry though that was often hard, and would have a sweet or savoury filling. A big effort went into our Christmas dinner; the aunties would be coming but not until 1 o'clock. We all had a good time, with lots of merriment including alcohol for the adults and juice for the children. John was not home much but when he was he could usually get a drink out of Dad, as it was Christmas.

Mam asked me to run upstairs to her room and get a dry towel; I moaned in my mind but did as I was told. Carol's towel was wet through, as she had splashed water when kicking her legs about. Mam said "You know there is lots to do today Marie I do need your help." I said "I know Mam, sorry."

In Mam's room there was a double bed and a set of drawers and wardrobe, and a cupboard over the stairs like George's room, which had all the towels in. Carol's crib was in the corner, I stood looking at it for a moment, the chamber pot, which we as children called a 'po', was just tucked under the bed. It had not been emptied and I saw floating on the top cigarette nubs where Dad had had a cigarette and put it out in his wee. I looked away in disgust, knowing it would be me that had to carry it to the toilet and empty it. I did it there and then to save me doing it later. I carried it very carefully trying not to get any on my hands. The toilet was two yards from Dad's door, just off the landing and next door there was a bathroom, which housed a steel bath, a sink and a huge wash basket, which was always overflowing.

Dad had stoked the downstairs fire up the night before, so in the morning he just raked all the dust out and stoked it up again. It was quicker than starting from scratch, then he transferred some hot coals into the fire grate in his bedroom, so his room was really warm, although it was just cinders now in the hearth. It was a warm room anyway due to the fact it had the boiler in the corner in a cupboard and the room was above the lounge, which nearly always had a blazing fire.

The fire downstairs was backed right up with logs and bits of coal around the edges; the fireguard was there to stop any fire rolling off onto the hearth. The room would stay warm both night and day, providing we had coal.

Chapter Five

Disappointed

I bolted down the stairs for the second time. I saw James and Robert undoing their presents, and putting mine to one side. There was Christmas paper all around the tree, and June was lifted out the bath and wrapped in the towel, dried and was dressed identical to Carol. I asked, "Mam can I look at my presents now?" She made an arm gesture so I scanned the room but I could not see my dolls house anywhere. Must be in the other room I thought. I ran past Mam, through two doors to where the table was but I could not see it anywhere. My heart sank. I knew it was not small and almost impossible to wrap. Then it suddenly occurred to me, my friends could be right there were too many of us. Trying hard not to cry I said, "Where is it? Where is it James? Stop playing tricks on me." James was always doing that; he hid things from me just to torment me. He asked, "What are you looking for?" "My dolls house." "I have not seen it Marie honest I haven't." Mam looked sad, "Sorry, Marie not this year." I stood in shock staring at the tree. Then I cried "But Santa said, and I prayed didn't I James? I prayed every night; I have been a good girl and helped you all the time. You even said I was your right arm, and that you could not manage without me, you said that Mam, you said "Maybe," Mam you said you would try, I always help you! Don't I Mam, don't I?"

"Mam! Please Mam tell me where have you hid it, stop joking, are you saving it until the aunties come?"

Mam carried on dressing June, ignoring my tantrum, and then she said, "Marie you have not got a dolls house, not this year. Now stop shouting as you will wake Carol and upset the others."

I was devastated, my Christmas was ruined and so was my faith, in both Santa and God. I was only a young child but I really believed God answered all prayers. I heard once in a sermon in church, you should never stop praying, the same prayer until it is answered. God says bring it to me in a prayer, God always answers a prayer, I did not know God answered prayers in his time, not ours, I learnt that much later in life. God had no concept of time. There were no calendars or clocks in Heaven.

Santa was so convincing, he had said I would get a dolls house, I will never believe in him anymore, My friends were right, it was just a story. Dad walked in the room; I looked at Mam and shouted at her "I hate you all, why did you have so many of us?"

Dad said "What's all this about?" Mam looked very sad, I saw tears in her eyes and I knew she felt my sadness. She said to Dad "I told you so; you just won't listen will you?" I could not hear everything that was being said after that because I was sobbing so loud. I only wanted a dolls house, I did not think for one minute I would not get one. A hint of some kind might have eased my mind, but I really believed I was having one; perhaps I was stupid, just like my so-called friends said.

Dad said that I had upset everyone else, ruined everyone's Christmas all because I was too selfish but this only made me cry more. I shouted "Susan was right, we have too many in our family that's why Santa only brings us small things." Dad asked, "Who the hell is Susan? She seems to be mentioned a lot in this house." I told him she was a girl at school who has a dolls pram and lots of games to play with and that she doesn't have any babies to look after. He looked away angrily and said, "You do not get everything you ask for my girl, and now you listen to me I am your Father you will not be cheeky to me or your Mother. Prayers are not answered, there is no one listening to you when you pray every night. God, Jesus whatever you want to call him only exists in storybooks, Jesus Christ, who fills her with all this rubbish? She's not going to that damn church anymore, and she is not playing with that Susan either have I met this girl? We should all be grateful we have anything at all, we have a new baby, what better gift can come into a family." I replied in a sob, feeling terrible at what I had said, "I know that and she is lovely" but what I said and what I was thinking were two different things. I kept my thoughts to myself, she is a real baby, I already had one of those with June and she was lovely too but I wanted a dolls house.

I helped Mam as much as I could but I was a child too at just seven and a half and I wanted to play with toys, anything other than real babies. Instead of playing, I was changing nappies and entertaining babies, I fed and watched them when Dad was in the pub and Mam went around to the neighbours for a cup of tea and a gossip for a break from the babies or when she went to bingo at the Adelphi in Bulwell. I washed them, got them dressed, took them to the park, I put them to bed, later when I was older I took them to school. I was at school myself and doing homework in between when did I play, but I was selfish they said, and I felt really guilty for my feelings. All I wanted was my dream dolls house, nothing else mattered, I made some furniture for it, look Dad I made the furniture for it sobbing even louder and at that moment I heard another Christmas carol on the television.

"Away in a manger, no crib for a bed.
The little Lord Jesus lay down his sweet head."

I shouted in anger "If God is not real why is it on the television and why do we have Christmas? Tell me that! Christmas is when baby Jesus was born; it's his birthday look it's on the telly." Dad shouted, "Turn that bloody rubbish off, there is no God, not in this house at any rate; Marie pack it up and stop being so selfish you ungrateful little sod or you will be in your bed for Christmas."

I ran upstairs crying and shouting "But there is a God, there is, at school in R.E. the teacher says there is, at church the vicar said there is, and why were you at church last night, what did you go there for? Why are you saying there is no God? He is all around us in whatever we do; I just know he is real." George bellowed, "Will you lot bloody shut up." I heard Mam say "She is not a baby anymore she is growing up, she understands more than you think, leave her for five minutes she will calm down, I will fetch her in a little while when the young uns are dressed."

Mam came upstairs to me and explained that money was tight, and encouraged me to join the others around the Christmas tree, I sobbed, "No, I hate Christmas and I hate God, and I hate Santa, and I know there is no Santa, but you said I have to believe for the young uns. Mam, am I being punished, punished for my sins?" She said, "I don't know what you mean, it's just a tantrum because you did not get what you ask for and we are sorry for that this has nothing to do with God."

Mam said, "Well at least you don't hate me do you?" I looked at her and she hugged me and I sobbed in her arms. Then I asked her if she was ill? She said, "No I have just had a baby, it makes you tired and sore, come down when you are ready Marie, we can still have a nice day and you do have some nice presents."

Mam left the room and went to the bathroom to get washed and dressed.

Dad worked hard, Mam had a lot on with seven of us, but my thoughts were horrible. *The fact he went straight to the pub several times a week did not seem reasonable. He could not raise the money to buy a dolls house because it was all behind the bar at the Red Lion, I even heard Mam say that. I suddenly realised I was being a really nasty person with all the nasty thoughts going around in my head, and I could not stop them. My head was full of anger, I began feeling a kind of hate towards my Dad, then my head disagreed, and I said sorry for my thoughts. I was feeling physical pain instead of just thinking, my body ached, I cried until I could no longer produce tears.*

Mam came in dressed in a maternity dress because she still had a very big tummy just 20 days after giving birth. She said "Sorry, I know you are disappointed Marie but if we had brought you a big gift the others would want one too, and we just could not afford anymore this year." She patted my shoulder then held my hand, "Come and see what we have brought for you." I remember her looking at me with tears in her eyes, I gave her half a smile, and she bent down and kissed me. I took her hand and we went down to the others.

Dad said I was a spoilt little brat because I was the first girl and that

I could not have everything I wanted. Mam told him to stop going on, Marie is alright now, Dad never ever smacked me, he only had to open his mouth in a stern voice and I was obedient to his requests, all his requests, whereas James got some good hidings, for doing nothing sometimes.

Times were hard with seven children to feed, though they made sure there was always a meal, in each of our bellies, something had to give. Mam passed me a gift, which I knew she had won at bingo, but that did not matter anymore we were mostly grateful for our gifts after all we did have some to undo. She went to bingo three times a week before Carol was born, and won lots of nice things and sometimes money. She worked two nights a week at the hospital as an orderly; she said she needed to go to bingo by way of a rest, from all us children. We looked after each other really, we were always arguing and fighting but we loved each other. Mam said I know it's not the same Marie but I have dressed it in lovely clothes it's not a baby doll, it's grown up like you. I untied the gift, which was wrapped in snowman paper and tied with shiny red ribbon. I mumbled thank you in between my sobs and put the doll on the chair.

James was also disappointed but never said a word about it. He looked at the doll and picked it up he said "It's nice Marie, look its arms and legs move." He was trying to console me, and "I did not get the car I asked for either, perhaps Santa ran out" he said. I looked at him and said very softly so the others did not hear, "There is no Santa, and it's a story." "I know," he said, then said "It's alright Marie maybe next year you will have your prayers answered." He was being nice to me and I appreciated that. He touched my hand with affection and I smiled at him; he handed me the doll "Look you can change her clothes." The doll was dressed in a pink hand knitted polo neck jumper and mini skirt to match; it even had crocheted pants and boots. Mam was so clever at knitting; she had put poppers on all the clothes so they could be changed or washed. James told me if you undo your other gifts you will find more clothes, I saw Mam knitting them. I sniffed hard and dried my eyes. I opened another gift and just as James had said there were more dolls clothes, a pair of navy blue trousers and another round neck jumper in lemon with short sleeves, a pale blue cardigan with lemon stripes to match, with a scarf and pom pom hat in navy, all hand knitted or crocheted by Mam.

CHAPTER SIX

CAROL SINGING

It was still Christmas morning when James was talking to me in the back room where the table was and baby Carol lay in the corner in her pram fast asleep. Mam and Dad were listening in the kitchen, as he explained to me why we sometimes did not get what we asked for. We were both upset, but I did not really understand money, and I cried on and off until something else took my mind off my disappointment. I thanked Mam for my gifts. Mam had knitted us all new jumpers or cardigans and they were wrapped up, as gifts so were John's and George's. They were too old for toys. Dad also had a jumper wrapped up, and although we had watched her knitting them all throughout the year it was still fun to unwrap the gift. They were called Aran cardigans, mine had buttons with a ballerina on, James' was the same but had a zip up the front and his design was a train. George had an eagle on the back of his. A lot of work went into them and we also had a woolly hat, gloves and a pair of socks.

On the nights leading up to Christmas James and I had joined with a lad named Alan and a few others to go carol singing around to the neighbours, and further afield if Mam was not in. We were able to buy gifts for Mam and Dad with the money, and if we went to the right houses we would get a tidy sum of money. Sometimes the people would give us sweets or an orange, sometimes a penny or sixpence and sometimes a shilling. Our theory was if the house had nice Christmas lights outside in a porch or on a tree in the garden, they were considered to be well off, and we were not very often wrong. Hard times but good as well, Mam said it was begging but she never stopped us going around local neighbours because everyone knew us. People would warm to me and James as we stood in the freezing cold all dressed up with hats and scarves and usually a torch and a song sheet, which we had stolen from church. It was full of Christmas carols and we would always sing at least one song all the way through and finish by singing We Wish you a Merry Christmas.

James had a good voice and mine was not that bad either so together with a few others we sounded pretty good or so we thought. Different people told us we sounded nice. Because we actually finished a song, when some kids only sang a line then hammered on the door, the neighbours would give generously and would often ask us in to sing for their family. We would then be given homemade mince pie or sausage roll and a drink and even money as well. They said to me, "Make sure that money treats your Mam" and we would always say, "Yes we will," and we did save most of the money for gifts. I remember we bought a nice cup and saucer for Mam, I still have it to this day and pipe cleaners for Dad or just chocolate if times were hard, we lived in a friendly neighbourhood. I think they felt sorry for us, and who wouldn't with seven children in one family.

Mam and Dad knew I would get over my disappointment, and did not pay too much attention to me. I was broken hearted but I had to show my gratitude for the gifts I had been given and I was grateful. I had set my heart on something I was sure to get, but not this Christmas.

The turkey was in the oven and Dad passed Mam a sherry and said "Happy Christmas." We were now all washed and dressed. James and I played with our gifts. James had a truck from one of the aunties and I had a sparkly purse with a clip fastener, not that I would ever have any money to put in it. There was sixpence inside as you always put money in a new purse. I liked it and put some of my little treasures in it. I liked saving buttons all different colours and shiny ones too; they were my treasures along with Mam's broken beads and trinkets. Each child had one main gift from Mam and Dad and a selection box, plus our new clothes, which we all wore on Christmas Day including our new cardigans. Although it was too hot to wear Aran cardigans in the living room near the fire, we needed them in the rest of the house because the coal fire was the only source of heat.

The selection box was for the afternoon, but Mam always let us eat a little chocolate and a few sweets from our selection box for breakfast as dinner would not be for hours and it was still only Christmas morning. The kitchen was full of prepared but uncooked dinner, and there would be a lot of dinner. Our aunties would bring their gifts with them when they arrived for dinner. They always gave nice gifts, usually clothes but nice ones. As they had no children of their own they would spoil us. James and I always received the same gift except his was for a boy and mine was for a girl, generally underwear and socks. I would also get a petticoat, a nightgown, a game and another selection box, which was a lot. The other auntie would buy a dressing gown and maybe slippers or a nice jumper and a toy or game. Often the same toy or game would be given every Christmas but we didn't mind as it was another present for us to open. We would sometimes hold our own fashion show in the living room wearing our new clothes.

CHAPTER SEVEN

CHRISTMAS DINNER

Dinner on Christmas Day was at the table in the front room. Again there was a fire in the grate though not as big as the fire in the living room but it warmed the room efficiently. The room was all dressed up with a small tree, which the children decorated themselves. It looked really pretty although we did not have any lights on it because Dad could not make the set work. The table was laid with a space for us all to sit. There were napkins at the side of each plate, and a candle stood proud in the centre of the table. There was a matching wine glass at each plate where the adults were to sit, and a plastic cup for the children, and a high chair for baby June. I gave Carol her bottle before we had our dinner and laid her in her carrycot where she gurgled and chanted and soon fell to sleep. The table looked good, warm and inviting, and the smell of the food was lovely. I absolutely loved Christmas and still do.

The aunties arrived, giving us all our presents. We could not open them until after dinner, except one, which we sneaked open while everyone was busy. The aunties had a glass of sherry to begin the festive cheer. George was up now and had a beer with Dad and the uncles. Dad always carved the turkey at the head of the table; with his ale in his hand he would say "Merry Christmas to one and all." There was a bottle of wine on the table for those who preferred it to ale and everyone returned the toast. The turkey would be served, adults first then the children, I just loved to have a wing with the crispy skin attached. The table soon looked a mess with the odd spilt drink, gravy and vegetables. There were always gravy spots dotted around the small amount of space there was left on the table after all the plates and vegetable dishes had been put in place. It did not really matter, today was Christmas Day and everyone was happy and getting merry with the alcohol which was flowing freely. Then we would pull the crackers with the silly jokes inside and the small plastic shapes, which sometimes resembled something. Sometimes no one could recognise what it was, but there was a hat for each of us in all-different colours. We would swap them about so we had one to match our outfits and there we sat forgetting the ordinary days gone by, just focusing on the moment, and we were happy.

Dad would put shiny new sixpences into the Christmas pudding, which he would make weeks before Christmas in a huge plastic bowl. I would have helped to make the pudding by stirring all the ingredients together, and then he would put the mixture into smaller basins ready for steaming. Dad poured brandy on to the sizzling pudding and lit it with a match; the flames would flare up in red and blue colours and then fizzle out. It was good fun if you found a sixpence. You had to make a wish and be careful not to swallow it and choke. The pudding was served with custard and a blob of very lumpy clotted cream, which was yellow in colour with a hard crust on top. Not many of us liked it, but Dad did, and so did I. It was sent by post from Plymouth and it came in a tin by special delivery from Dad's family.

We all helped clear the table, creating mountains of pots which James and I had to do. We always fell out over who was drying the pots, neither of us like drying, we never did pans though; they were left and Dad did them later. There was a giant pan into which leftover food went. In fact anything that was left on the table or even on the plates, if it had not been chewed, went in that pan. There were always lots of potatoes left which would go into a different pan with the vegetables for a fry up on Boxing Day. This was served with cold turkey and piccalilli or homemade tomato chutney and pickled onions which Dad had pickled in the weeks previous.

Even the carcass from the turkey went into the pan of leftovers. Dad would say there is lots of meat hiding on a carcass and every last bit would be boiled off. It would feed us all for several days. That same turkey would be used in many different disguises; the bulk of the leftover meat might be made into a pie or a stew. The carcass and scraggy ends would be made into soup. Over the next week we would eat leftover turkey and ham in one form or another. The mince pies never seemed to run out because Dad made hundreds of them and when they went hard we had them with custard.

Christmas was a time of good food and there appeared to be plenty of it but we all knew that January would be very different. It was our hardship month. Some days we didn't know if we would get a main meal, we didn't have a fridge or freezer so what food was in the cupboard was soon used up.

After everything settled down we unwrapped our gifts from the aunties, this particular Christmas James had a shirt and a bow and arrow and I had some nice knickers and a pair of thick tights, a nightgown and a board game. The black and white television got switched on and Dad would snooze in the chair, whilst Mam and the aunties chatted. We would all be told to play outside for an hour or two and we went back in at 4 o'clock when it was getting dark. All the adults had lots to drink and they were snoozing by the firelight.

Christmas was soon over; no dolls house that year. Life soon went back to normal, all the Christmas cheer had gone and now we had the aftermath to deal with, the cleaning and putting away all the trimmings and putting the best set of plates back in the cabinet. We knew normality had returned because Mam and Dad started arguing again about money. He said Mam spent too much on gifts and Mam would say he spent too much on food and booze. Mam very rarely drank alcohol so she did have a valid point. Nevertheless there was always a very bad atmosphere during January and the kids were stuck in the middle again.

Chapter Eight

The Wedding

During the following summer I was to be a bridesmaid to one of my cousins. I went for several dress fittings so the beautiful pink-layered dress fitted to perfection. It was not a long dress to the floor like I expected. It finished just below the knee and had lots of net underskirts, which made it stand out like a ballerina dress. I had to wear white lacy ankle socks and white ballerina shoes which Mam bought from the wishing book. My hair would be curled into lots of ringlets at the hairdressers. It was pinned with pink and white daisy flowers around the crown of my head. I was very excited and looking forward to dressing up in my new best dress.

A few weeks before I was to be a bridesmaid I was sent home from school with a letter but instead of going straight home to Aunt Bess' house, I had to go to my friend's house next door. Aunt Bess was going to be late home and had asked my friend's Mam to look after me for half an hour. My friend's Mam took the letter off me and opened it; I did not care what the letter was about as I was too young to be bothered. After she read the letter she turned to me and said "Come here you, do you know you have lice in your head?" I had long hair with a little wave running through it; I had it tied in a ponytail at the back. I replied, "No I haven't." She said, "That's what the letter says." I got really upset and was told "Play in the garden and don't go near each other and don't share hats and clothes." When Aunt Bess came home my friend's Mam took me round and stood with the letter in her hand and pushed it into Aunt Bess' hand. "Here this is for you and I don't want her to come around here again until they're gone." Aunt Bess opened the letter and looked at me saying, "Go inside

Marie." I don't know what they said to each other but I know they never spoke to each other ever again and I was never allowed to go to my friend's house to play.

The lice and nits presented a massive problem as my hairstyle for the wedding had been carefully planned. As soon as she read the letter Mam whisked me straight down the hairdresser and said "Off with the lot, chop it all off." The hairdresser said, "There is some spirit you can put on the hair which you leave on overnight; it kills the lot" but Mam said "No cut it all off." I sat there watching as my locks fell to the floor, I was in tears; the hairstyle ended up just below my ears and cut straight across at the back. For two weeks after my hair had been cut off I had to endure the daily routine of Mam using the fine-toothed nit comb on what was left of my hair. Mam used the comb so rigorously it scratched my scalp until it bled but Mam continued using it until I was completely free of nits and lice. My hair has always had a bald patch where the follicles had been damaged from that occasion.

When my lice and nits had completely gone James got them; they went through the family like the plague, back and forth from one to another, we all had short hair that year and visited the nit nurse weekly for the smelly lotion to be rubbed onto our scalp, everyone knew we had the nits.

My cousin was not very happy that I had my hair cut short but she still allowed me to be her bridesmaid, what else could she do? I already had my best new pink-layered dress and all the nice accessories. After the nits I came down with terrible sore throats one after the other, and was quite ill with them, but got over them in time for the wedding for them to return afterwards.

Dad's attention to me, it was growing ever stronger, a strange kind of attention that made me feel uneasy.

Chapter Nine

JOHN

A whole year was drifting by, the snow had gone then the spring then summer and here was autumn around again. The year had brought me more misery but the secret was safe, I told no one.

After school Mam would give the youngest their tea and sit James, Robert and me on her knee, and June was tucked under there somewhere as well. She wrapped a blanket around us all and we sat in the firelight, as there was no money for the electricity, she would tell us ghost stories until Dad got home, or until bedtime whichever came soonest, Carol was already tucked up in bed. The story went like this;

There was a dark dark road with a dark dark house
And in the dark dark house was a dark dark room
And in the dark dark room was a dark dark cupboard
And in the dark dark cupboard was a GHOST

She would shout it so loud we nearly jumped out of our skins. We were all scared but did not let on. We would say "Say it again, say it again," Mam would tell the story just once more. Then she would show us some animals on the wall, and with great precision she would move her fingers to look like rabbit ears, and many other animals. In the light of the fire animals appeared in shadows on the wall; it was magic.

I had seen another dolls house in the wishing book which started me off again, I said "Mam what about this Christmas?" She said, "Not out of that book it is too much money," I know she ordered out of the catalogue often. It was a catalogue where you paid weekly, except Mam would fall behind with the payments. Then she and Dad would fall out and shout, but because he was at work and then off to the pub Mam said he did not understand her needs trying to bring the family up. The row would get bigger and shouting get louder until Mam backed down crying. Anything that was of value was sent back to the wishing book which meant Mam got the debt down and our favourite gifts were no more. That is why I asked Santa if he took gifts back 2 weeks after Christmas. Cruel as it seemed we got used to it but little did I know how it would have a lasting effect on our memories it was indeed a cruel thing to happen to a child a little like giving you a lollipop just to snatch it away after the first lick. Mam called it the wishing book because we would say Mam wish we could have this or wish we could have that. Sometimes we kids would fall out with each other because boys and girls sections would be on different pages so we would end up in a scrap until Mam took it off us. Then we would come back later and start again and say the same, and add on other things until we ran out of pages. Mam would let us all wish our way through the toy section because that's what they were, just wishes. But Mam did her best, and we were usually grateful for anything new.

As I mentioned earlier John joined the navy in 1966, beginning his career on a ship on May 12th my birthday. He looked so handsome in his white navy uniform. He began his career as a steward. I was so proud to call him my brother I wrote him letters and enjoyed receiving them back it was just chit chat usually about how I was doing at school and how all the family was, I loved him coming home on leave, which was not as often as I would have liked. He brought us gifts from foreign countries like from China a Chinese silk dressing gown it was bright red with gold embroidered dragons that told a story all around the gown it had tiny fabric covered buttons and little loops as button holes and a mandarin neck line it was beautiful I wore it until it fell into shreds where I dare not have it washed for fear of losing it. One time he gave me a Seiko watch from Japan, which I still have today, it still works just fine. They were very special gifts and meant the world to me always unusual and nice. But John meant more to me more than any of the gifts and I longed for him to be home so we could chat I longed to tell him my secret but dare not.

I remember I had a postcard, which came in an envelope, which was real kangaroo fur. I know now it was very cruel but at the time I thought it was so precious I never thought about a kangaroo being killed just for its fur. I hoped it came from a dead animal on the roadside, I would feel it and then put it away safely in its tissue in my shoebox of treasures until I felt lonely or scared again then in my thoughts it would bring John home to me safely and I would get it out and feel it once again. I suppose in a way that kangaroo did not die in vain because it brought me such comfort in my time of need.

John was my inspiration and encouragement because he treated me like a real person; I was not a Mam to the young uns or a slave to him. He was my brother and I was his sister, he would take me into Nottingham in my best dress he made me feel so grown up and yet treated me like a kid sister a time to let go of my abuse and relax and laugh just for a day. Sometimes we would go to the Nottingham Castle and take photographs of buildings; he was always interested in photography. Then he would treat me to lunch he lit up my life when he came home on leave. I got really excited at the thought, sometimes he would say he was coming home but he didn't because he had his own life girlfriends and the like. I never understood that as I was too young, it made me very sad that he could not live with us when he came home. I know sometimes he stayed with my aunt in the pub and I wrote a letter to her saying she could not have him, or words to that effect. It did upset her but I needed my brother to talk to, to keep me sane, she said later in life I hurt her feelings by writing it but she did not know my reasons. Life is never simple; John came home with his own set of problems, which I did not know either until years later. He would drink himself into oblivion, and that's why he stayed away so often. I still think James and my life would have been different somehow, if John had stayed home because he cared about us and things would not have gone so far, though I could not know this for sure. I even cried because I looked forward to seeing him so much and he was the only person I felt close enough to share my secrets with. It never happened, it couldn't; I was so close to writing my secrets in a letter. I would begin writing then stop, because I knew of the pain I would cause all the others in the family.

I thought if I wrote my thoughts and feelings down in a letter to John it would not be like I was actually telling anyone so it would be all right. I did not know how John would react, but I knew the next time he came home on leave he would sort it out, as he would have to do the right thing by me. In the end I didn't send the letter because I knew what the consequences would be for my family and me when John went back to the navy. Telling John and letting him sort it out would not have stopped my pain. In fact it would almost certainly have made the situation worse and I would have to live with it for the rest of my life. My secret was bad enough and hard to live with but I couldn't put the rest of my family through the pain I was feeling. I was only a child and yet I knew what was happening to me had to stay a secret.

CHAPTER TEN

LITTLE GEM

Christmas was again on the horizon but this year I decided not to pray to God for anything in particular as it didn't do me any good last year and I didn't even want to see Santa. And although I still prayed I did not really believe my prayers would be answered, I was told there was no such man as Santa and that Mam and Dad bought our gifts, so the large family theory was true enough. It all seemed to make sense now, the fewer the number of children the better the gifts. I must sound very ungrateful but when you are told by your pals and older members of the family time after time it seems to penetrate your head, just like when they constantly call you stupid or thick eventually you begin to believe you really are. Anyway, ungrateful or not I was not expecting much in the way of gifts as Mam was getting worse with her illness. After the year we had gone through we were still looking forward to Christmas, I enjoyed all the fuss and the family coming together and the whole family needed to be cheered up. Although there was nothing catastrophic that happened, Mam was very unhappy and it rubbed off on everyone; she was our Mam after all. She had lots of days when she did not feel well I would hear her sobbing in the bedroom and she was planning another hospital stay. We came to understand she was sick, but she told us nothing, no one did, as we were too young to understand she said. She just said she needed extra help from me that went without saying, I helped as much as I could before school I dressed the young un's, Dad cooked the porridge, we all went to school & nursery at the weekends or even in the early evening after school I cleaned, cooked, scrubbed the quarry tiled kitchen floor on my hands and knees I was

42

a very young age I ironed straight things like tea towels and pillow cases and looked after the young un's I made cakes too Mam was so proud of me she took some of the cakes around to the neighbours so they could taste them. The neighbours would say you have a little gem there it's a good job you have her to help you I heard one say God gave her that girl to help her in her time of need though at the time I never knew what they meant.

I heard Mam say John was coming home for Christmas so I got very excited. I made him a special Christmas card. John had helped me learn my times table. In our letters he said say them before you go to bed, keep writing them down whenever you can and I was ready to recite them to him; one time he was home he helped me look in the correct books for homework projects and he took me to the library and taught me to find books as the library was so confusing, he also said don't pull yourself down you are as good as all the others he gave me a feeling of self worth if only I could believe it, of course I never did believe it.

CHAPTER ELEVEN

SHOOTING

Mrs Ward the neighbour next door gave Mam lots of oddments of wool, which she saved over time, from knitting cardigans for us, which were great for making dolls clothes. She would also give the children apples and oranges for going to the grocery van for her. Sometimes she only wanted a packet of biscuits, but still gave us a treat. James and I would take it in turns. When the van came on the street, we would rush around to knock on the door. We knew what sharing meant, we were inseparable and we went everywhere together. When James' friends weren't there we had a special bond due to our ages being so close, we played and chatted just like we were twins and we were often treated like twins. When one had new shoes the following week the other got a pair. Mam and Dad could only afford cheap plastic jellybean shoes and we all had Wellington boots, as they got passed from one of us to another. If we had no shoes we wore the Wellies and if we had none that fit us, the church had regular jumble sales, which Mam would go to with all the young uns in tow.

Between you and me, Mam got half the stuff free because the church people felt sorry for her with four young children in tow. It was the same with the butcher down the road when Mam bought Dad his meat; he always gave me a raw sausage to eat on the way home. They were made of fresh pork in those days not full of fat I hungrily squashed it out of its skin and ate it raw, Mam used to say you will get worms or the trots eating it raw, but I don't remember ever being ill through them. I suppose it was because it was all fresh meat, not filled with additives like these days.

The neighbours up and down the road were very good to us all, as well as our Mam who would often be found sitting in a neighbour's house drinking tea, because the electric meter had ran out of money. There was always a fire in the hearth as the coal came from the coal mine, where Dad had an allowance of coal, which came in bags and had to be counted off the lorry. They always came early in a morning and Mam would say to look out the window and count the bags coming off the lorry just in case the men who delivered it were on the fiddle. They would hold a bag or two back and flog it on. Mam would also let her friend take a bag occasionally when we had plenty and they had none. You shared with your neighbours in those days because you never knew when you would need help yourself, but if the cold weather was prolonged, we would definitely run out of coal and because everyone was in the same boat, there was no coal anywhere on the street no matter how good the neighbour was. The house would become really freezing in no time at all, especially if they had no money to buy any from the shop, we already had our coats on the beds and one grey or brown very prickly army blanket very rough to the skin but we had to keep warm so no one moaned.

Coal was not cheap from the local shop, money was tight and it would have to be carried or collected in the pram. We would use the bits right down to the gravel slack at the bottom of the bunker and after the delivery men had gone Mam sent us onto the road to pick up all the lumps of coal which had fallen from the lorry, it was like gold dust. Dad or George would sometimes bring home a tree from the woods at the viaducts on the way to Bulwell where they went shooting for pigeons. I never really knew where or what the viaducts were until much later. Dad took the dog and me with him one day it was good fun running in the tall grass, the viaducts were huge arched bridges all joined together; there must have been at least 6 of them Dad said they were the strongest type of bridge and that train tracks ran across the top of them we could hear the trains shooting by like noisy dragons flying over us. Woods surrounded the bridges, and lots of swampy grass areas were all around us; there were water reeds and there was dense undergrowth and a few patches of very tall grassland. It covered a large area but as I was only small it probably appeared much more vast than it actually was. Dad would shoot the big wood pigeons some of them were as big as a duck and even looked like ducks to me, once he knew he had hit one he would then send the dog to collect it and when he had 4 or 5 we would leave for home, whilst we walked up the hill Dad would talk of the lovely pie which he would make for supper but before that he had to pluck the birds and clean them they stank horrid but once in the pastry tasted really nice. Dad tried to teach me but I never could pluck or skin an animal or bird, I just could not tackle that job.

Washday was always Mondays; Mam would be washing the clothes all day in a rented twin tub washing machine. The washing was hung right up the garden and back down again, on two huge washing lines with two or three props made of wood which Dad had made out of lengths of rough wood they were so heavy I could hardly lift them. The wash basket was never empty with all our lot, and as I got older on rainy days the washing was my job. With so many of us Mam had all on keeping the house tidy, and the ironing hardly ever got done? It just got ironed as and when we needed our clothes and Mam had already taught me how to iron shirts you just iron the collar and the bit at the front she would say Marie no one sees the back and if it was cold and they were wearing a jumper I only ironed the collars, I never iron underwear, towels, sheets in-fact whatever we could get away with never got ironed jeans got ironed occasionally so I was taught how to fold with precision so clothes did not need ironing, my brothers took advantage of the fact I could iron they would say Marie iron this for me I sometimes got a few sweets but if I refused I got a thump. The neighbours would say a regular little housewife Marie is getting or she will make someone a good wife when she marries. She is so good to those babies too; we have never seen her without one attached to her hip. Sometimes they would say where's yer Mam? I see you have got the young uns again I would just ignore their comments, and think nosey old crows what's it got to do with you. Mam told me off she said I should not use bad language that I would never be a lady, I had visions of me dying at a young age as all girls grew up to be women and a lady was just another word for it. What did she mean?

Other sayings were

(Bread and if it's) she said that if we asked what's for tea. (If it's there you can eat if it's not you can't

Or (Bread and same) which was Bread on one side and same on the other.

Or (A walk around the table.

Or (I'll smack your arse if you fall down) like you fell down on purpose.

Or (If you ask you won't get it for asking, but if you don't ask you won't get it because I will not know you won't it.) Make sense of that one, in other words you cannot have it either way.

My Mam had a lot of sayings like that, none of which really made sense.

CHAPTER TWELVE

HOLIDAY CAMP

In the summer of 1963 Mam needed to have a serious operation, she would be in hospital for two to three weeks, so it was arranged for June who was only 2 to go into a foster care home, Robert went to stay with a neighbour Mrs Johnson, Carol who was still a new baby stayed with Mam and Dad, James and I went to Skegness holiday camp for deprived children for two weeks, Dad's pit paid for this from the benevolent fund, this was a scheme into which employees paid a small amount of money out of their wages, that went into a central fund. If your family met the criteria it enabled the family to claim money for different needs like my brother and I going to a holiday camp whilst Mam was ill.

The first thoughts in my mind were Mam and Dad did not want us anymore. We did not realise it was for just two weeks, we never got told anything, it was on a 'need to know' basis and Dad said we did not need to know. I wondered if I had let out my secret without knowing maybe in my sleep or someone could tell by my demeanour, my mind once again began going into overdrive. Perhaps others had found out somehow but that was not the case. It was genuinely because Mam was ill and needed some peace and quiet, we were told that when we got back.

Mam bought us new underwear and socks, and a few other things to go with. She packed us a small case each; with the few clothes we took folded neatly on one side, and a towel and wash bag on the other.

We were a little excited and somewhat apprehensive, as we climbed the steps to the bus, with our suitcase having been stacked neatly in the boot that was under the bus, a large door seamed to come out the side to reveal a huge hollow space that held baggage.

As Mam waved goodbye with tears in her eyes, I shed a few tears but they soon dried up as I tried to think of this as a huge adventure just James and me, I think I was more excited than James. It was a new experience going on a bus on our own with new places to see and explore. James and I sat together and I was chatting most of the way not knowing what to expect.

When we arrived at our destination we both got up to get off the bus, and a voice said "WO! Not you young lady, this is the boys' camp"; I said "What camp? What do you mean we are having a holiday whilst our Mam is in hospital?" The man said "But not to-gether young lady" and he gave a chuckle, which made me feel uneasy. James looked around at me, I will never forget his face although he was not crying, because that would have looked sissy in front of the other boys but I could tell he was crying inside, and so was I. My heart was screaming inside *where are you taking my brother? Camp, what camp? James, is it for naughty boys and girls? What did we do so wrong to have to go to a camp? I had wanted to be with James, why couldn't we be together? Dad always said if I told anyone, I would go into a home for naughty girls but I had told no one about my secret so why the camp, I thought our Mam was ill.* James and I had no idea we were being split up. There were just girls left on the bus, no one spoke to me or even looked at me come to that. Mam had dressed me in a blue and white gingham dress, a hand knitted cardigan in navy with new white socks and sandals. I had my hair in two bunches, one either side of my head, each bunch tied with a blue ribbon. Mam had made the effort to make us look smart. It was summer and very warm and the other girls looked quite normal to me, dressed a little better than me perhaps, as my new dress looked the same as the one I had to wear for school as part of my summer uniform, and in fact later it would become just that.

One girl had scabs all around her lips and chin, her hair was a little bedraggled and she sat alone. I did not know then but I would later befriend her. Another girl was really pretty with long blonde wavy hair, she was wearing a pretty blouse with pink flowers all over it and a gathered shirt, which was plain pink. It looked like a suit fit for a wedding, she looked so smart, and I heard her say her name was Fiona. She was talking constantly to a girl who was sat at the side of her; I think they call it 'verbal diarrhoea'. She did not come up for air; nor did she wait for an answer to her questions. The girl who was listening had her haircut nearly to her scalp and was dressed like a boy, with a blue shirt and grey school trousers. She had a sallow look, a sad look; she said her name was Tina. I wondered what her problem was. It seemed at this point we all had reasons for being there, all had some secret to share, but could we trust each other? Not at this point anyway.

The blonde girl Fiona, who talked a lot, was saying this was her third time at camp and that her parents were splitting up, there was a court case with both parents arguing over who she was to live with. Her Mam lived in the Far East, and her Dad lived in England. Both her parents were very influential important business people. She did not seem to mind which parent won custody of her, she said because both were rich and that she had them both wrapped around her little finger, and whatever she asked for she got. She then proceeded to get her purse out her very nice pink handbag. Was she bragging about how much money she had? *Why was she here, with what appeared to be children, with no money and not well off at all and most from large families as far as I could gather. If she is loaded why hasn't she gone somewhere posh, or stayed with her nanny, whom she talked about? Again my thoughts were in overdrive.* At that point I lost interest in her one sided conversation, which was loud enough for the whole bus to hear. I just sat staring out of the bus window, at the places we passed. It seemed ages since we dropped off the boys; we were a long way from their camp. I said a little prayer, Lord Jesus bring my brother James back to me safely. The bus screeched and pulled up at some big iron gates, which could have been from a horror film. The gates opened with a button and intercom. I felt fear building inside my stomach and felt a little nauseous. We were told to get off the bus and collect our cases and bags from the hold under the bus.

We were directed through a playground into a large building and were ushered into a huge room with rows of wooden tables and benches. The floor was grey and everywhere looked cold and uninviting. A tall, quite fat woman with grey curly hair and hands the size of shovels, wearing a dark grey dress and black lace up shoes, introduced herself as matron. She told all of us to take a seat, and leave our bags and cases where they were and sit at a bench. There were twelve of us in total so we shuffled to sit on the long wooden benches either side of the huge wooden table.

We were served with plate thick bread coated in dripping; it was white dripping lard with brown jelly marbled through it. I overheard Fiona saying to matron I do not eat this, Mummy said I was to tell you, may I have cheese? The matron nodded to another person in the kitchen, and minutes later she came out with a cheese sandwich, cut into four pieces, I was used to eating dripping at home so I tucked in, I sprinkled mine with salt. It was quite edible and no one else complained but the faces they pulled told if they had eaten bread and dripping before. I just ate it, as I did not know the consequences if I didn't and I was hungry, and then jugs of weak orange cordial were put on the table for us to help ourselves.

Our ages differed somewhat from about 7 to 11 years old. I was 9 and although I was terrified, I began to relax a little. I was daydreaming with the cup of juice in my hand, thinking *when will I be going home, I wonder where James is, have we really been that naughty? Although that thought was going through my mind, I was sure Fiona had not been bad, she seemed a little too proper for that, so why had Mam sent us away? Maybe she didn't love us anymore, we had no explanation. Am I to live on dripping I wondered?*

A loud bang on the table at the side startled me. "What did I just say young lady?" I jumped, almost spilling my drink. I looked up at the matron and nodded in the direction of I don't know and I shrugged my shoulders at the same time. "Did anyone else not hear what I said?" Everyone stayed quiet while she made me stand up and say what I thought she might have said. I mumbled I don't really know, as I was thinking of my Mam. The matron shouted "Speak up girl." I said even louder, "I don't know, I don't know what you said." She shouted "Well we have a right one here, haven't we girls? Firstly you must listen otherwise you will not know what to do next will you? And secondly you refer to me as Matron; otherwise it's going to be a long two weeks for you my girl and that goes for you all."

I breathed a sigh of relief as she said two weeks, I replied yes matron, sorry matron. I will try to listen matron but not daring to look into her eyes as I felt I would be turned into stone if I did. Then all at once she said "Look at me when I am speaking to you girl," then matron smirked at me, looking around as she was creating an audience with all the girls in the room. She looked directly into my face and said "For your punishment you will clear the table when we have finished supper." I replied, "Yes matron," and *thought well at least I know what to do; I was quite at home clearing up.* I felt that matron could read my mind. She was very bossy, then she said "Did you mutter something girl?" And again I shook my head and swallowed the bread in my mouth. There was some bread and dripping still on the plate and I was still hungry but whilst my stomach wanted more, my body did not react as I felt too scared to move, in case I upset matron again. The matron went on to tell us what time our meals would be and some rules and regulations and what she expected from us.

After her speech, she said "Will you all get your bags and follow me." I stayed behind and cleared the table as I was ordered to do; I piled up the plates and took them to the kitchen. Then the kitchen lady who did all the cooking introduced herself as Betty. Betty showed me the way to where the others were. As we walked along the long corridor she chatted non-stop to me hardly taking a breath. She said "You're a good little helper; I can tell you have cleared before." I never answered her, just in case I said the wrong thing she did seem nice but Dad said keep it zipped so I nodded politely. When we arrived in a huge room I looked down each side the room was lined with identical beds, identical covers all made with precision lined up like solders cold and uninviting. "This is the dormitory," Betty said. Betty had red coloured hair, which was thick and wavy, and she was wearing a white pinny, which covered all her clothes a bit like a dress over another dress. "Now go on catch up with the others and I will see you in the morning at breakfast." She tapped my bottom to scoot me along. I looked up at her rosy face and she smiled a kind smile, which was the only thing pleasant about this place up to now but it did help me relax a little.

Matron said, "Come and join us" and she asked what me name was. "It's Marie matron." "Now listen carefully," she said, "I was just saying you all have a set of drawers at the side of your bed, use them for underwear and socks. Each bed has a wardrobe, this has to be shared between two, I expect your beds to be made each morning, after the bell before you wash and dress, did you all hear me?" She looked directly at me, we all shouted "Yes matron."

Matron said to follow her and showed us into a washroom, which had three toilets each side, down the centre were six washbasins set into worktops, all had hot and cold taps. It all looked very old fashioned with green brick shaped tiles on the walls and quarry tiles on the floor. It was a cold room even though the day was warm; at the end were two baths. Her words seemed to echo in the stark room and became harsh again. "You must clean your bath after use, and believe me I will find out who left the mess. Now each of you find a bed and unpack, you can have an early night tonight as most of you have been travelling all day. Get to know your surroundings and your bed neighbour so you can remember which bed is yours. Any bed accidents must be reported to me, you will not be told off but you will be if you do not tell me. In the cupboard" she pointed her hand to the corner, "there are some books and a few games which you can use but put the games back after use each evening and you may keep the book in your bedside cabinet until you have read it. I will talk more tomorrow I think that is enough for now, goodnight" and away she went and closed the door behind her.

Fiona ran down the dormitory almost knocking another girl over, and jumped on a bed saying this is mine, I always sleep in the same bed. Come on Tina you can have this one next to me; we don't want to get her scabs. Tina followed her and then the scabby girl and I walked to the opposite side of the room and chose our beds. Her scabs did not bother me because when there were lots of family members there was always someone with either nits or scabs. I said to the scabby girl "My name is Marie" but she looked down at the floor. I said "Well what's your name?" She said "Carol, my name is Carol I am 9 how old are you?" "I'm 9 and I have a sister called Carol, what are the scabs on yer face, cold sores?" She answered "Yes, I often get them; I have to use my own towel." I said "Well they are not that bad they will soon go. Bet everyone calls you scabby at school don't they?" They were pretty bad all over the chin area, but I did not want her to feel too bad after all I needed a friend at the moment and I am not a cruel person. "Come on let's unpack, then we will go in the cupboard where matron said and see what is in there." We did just that then we talked about how she came to be there. Her Mam drank a lot of alcohol she said, and her Dad could not look after her and her other brothers and sister. They had all gone into foster homes though she did not say exactly that but, she said a woman took them away to live with other families, so I guessed it was the same as June. She told me over the week she used to get a beating off her drunken Mam and that her Mam and Dad used to fight with fists on occasions. I never shared my secret with her even though she had with me that made me feel bad. But I just couldn't, I could never share my secret, even though over the next 2 weeks our friendship grew and we might never meet again.

Carol and I went to the cupboard shelf to get a book, I chose a book called Lorna Doone, which I kept and read a few pages each night, I liked reading, some of this book was a little too hard for me, but I read most of it. I did not get the chance to read very often with all the jobs I had to do at home. I always remember reading Black Beauty. I loved that book and I had annuals for Christmas like Judy and Bunty.

We all seemed to pair up into couples, a sort of buddy thing, which was nice, Carol and I were partners in crime, so to speak. We got on really well and seemed to understand each other, she soon lost her shyness and we were inseparable. It seamed like we had known each other forever and learning of her situation made me feel humble and that my home life was not so bad after all or it could have been that I had empery rest bite from it.

I got ready for bed myself putting on me new pink nightgown that had embroidery along the bottom it was very pretty me Mam did me proud, We got into bed with a smile to each other. There was a thin cold cotton sheet covering the mattress and another one which went over me, and one grey brownish coloured blanket, with a thin striped bed-spread, which hung down the sides, and a small flat pillow. Though it was a warm summer it did seem cold in the dormitory so we snuggled down to get warm, I felt tiredness come over me, and said goodnight. It was dark and I wondered where I was and where my brother was. *I thought my prayers in my head as always;*

God bless all the family and especially James, God where is James, I hope he is all right, please let me know he is all right. The tears began to flow down my cheeks and I heard another girl crying out loud and Fiona shouted shut up think of it as an adventure a break from your family's'. She was right; really we were stuck here and could do nothing about it. It was ok really and the beds were clean and warm and we would get our meals I thought. I will talk to Betty tomorrow, she seemed approachable and nice, I will ask where James is, Yes that's what I will do. I never got to say the Lords Prayer I was drifting fast into to unconsciousness.

The next thing I knew a loud bell was ringing in my ears, everyone woke up startled, after all how could they sleep through that? We made our beds as instructed and went to the bathroom. I got the toothpaste out of my bag and all the girls looked at it, they all had tubes of toothpaste whilst I had a tin with a pink solid block of funny tasting toothpaste in it, which you had to rub your brush over. I have to admit I had never seen toothpaste like that before either. I just shrugged and got on with my teeth cleaning it was not bad once I got used to the taste. I had a nice new flannel and a bar of coal-tar soap, which really stank horrible, Carol offered me to use hers but the bar was only small and might not have lasted us both for two weeks so I declined the offer and she had all those scabs but it did smell nice. I heard Fiona again saying that's what poor families use. I felt like punching her she was asking for a good punch, having grown up with 4 brothers I knew how to look after myself and was not afraid of her. Mind you she was right it was horrible soap. We all did what we had to do and we went back to the dormitory and got ourselves dressed. I was sitting on my bed when a voice shouted, "Follow me," her voice seemed to ring in my ears like the bells from church on a Sunday morning.

We all assembled in a line and followed matron to the dining room. "Right take your places." Most of us sat in the place where we had sat the night before. Matron said "Our days are organised for us and breakfast was at 7.30 lunch was at 12.00 dinner was at 4.30 and supper was 7.00. We like you to eat the food put in front of you, as it's not cheap, and we do not like waste, so do not ask for more than you can eat, do you understand me?" We all nervously answered yes Matron and nodded at the same time.

"There are no chores to do here except your beds to make each morning, which I have mentioned, and the bathroom must be kept clean do not leave blobs of toothpaste all down the basin and hair dangling about. I will know which hair belongs to which head. I thought fat chance of my toothpaste on the basin mine is in a block that's one thing I cannot be accused of. If you misbehave then you get a punishment chore, you are here to enjoy yourselves so let's not have any of that she was glaring right at me." I blew out from my mouth maybe a little too loud wishing I hadn't. Matron said "Do you have something to say to us all Marie?" "No Matron." Phew I reckon she's gunning for me I thought.

Breakfast was porridge which I liked, others moaned but again I was used to it, I went to the counter and Betty smiled, "One or two scoops?" Remembering what matron said I said "One please," she quietly said "Come back if you are still hungry and if I have some left you can have some more." I replied "Thank you Betty." She did seem nice we seemed to get on, unlike the very strict matron.

The day was warm and matron said "Everyone outside, go and explore find your way around the garden and around the corner is a park with swings. In the corner are some very high trees do not climb them they are out of bounds. In one hour I will take you for a walk along the beach yes we will enjoy the fresh air today."

I hung back till the room was empty. I loaded some dishes into my hands and walked to the kitchen where Betty was, she said "You do not have to clear again it's my job." "Well Betty I need to ask you a question." "Go on then fire away." "Well my brother came with me and I wondered where he was?" "Why he'll be in the boy's camp; you might see him on your walk sometimes they have the same routines as us it being a nice warm summers day, I am sure you will bump into him on your walk to the beach." "But Betty is it the same as here?" "Yes pet he will make friends just like you will, now go and play, he's alright." She smiled and said "Go on then" and showed me outside, saying this is your little holiday, it's a holiday not a punishment, now go and make friends, don't mind me I will see you at lunch. I looked up at her face and said "Thank you". I ran out the door, where Carol was waiting for me. She was looking down at her shoes, she always hung her head low. I asked "What's up?" She said "Nothing." "Well come on then let's play." We ran to the swings and laughed as we kicked back and forth to go higher and higher. "I saw one of the lads from our school go right over the top bar have you ever seen that Carol?" Carol said "No we do not have a park near us we live in a block of flats so we do not even have a garden do you know what a flat is?" "Can't say as I do really." "We have to go to our home on a lift when it's working if it's broken down we climb hundreds and hundreds of steps do you have a garden Marie?" "Yes." Then remembering what Dad said about telling people our business I jumped off the swing and headed for the seesaw. Carol jumped off and sat on the other end where we went up and down and sang a daft song as we did it we both had a giggle and began to relax.

Another bell rang and we all lined up. I was so excited I might see James that I could hardly contain myself. We walked along the back road passing some railings like the ones we had around our garden. I told Carol about my brother whilst we were walking and when she saw some boys she nudged me, but it was not James. We had to walk fairly fast to keep up with matron. I was not enjoying my walk at all. My eyes were scanning every group of boys we saw, and matron caught me lagging behind. "Catch up Marie I do not want to lose you. The walk was supposed to be fun," she said. The same routine went on for a few days and then when we were playing on the beach with a ball there was a bunch of boys, and James was there among them. I ran over and said "Hey James are you okay?" He held out his hand and said "Yes are you?" Both our group leaders shouted ready to leave. We both walked in different directions. "We have to go, bye James it's just 2 weeks, James not for ever like we thought, Betty the cook said two weeks that's all." He shouted "Bye Marie" as we walked away in different directions. There was a couple lying on the beach with a radio on, it was playing a song by Brian Hyland, "And it's going to be a long lonely summer". The tears flooded down my face as I caught up to the others. Carol said "You okay Marie?" I wiped my eyes and said "Yes come on." "Was that yer brother Marie do yer get on with him?" I was not sure how to answer so I just gave a halfhearted smile, and hurried to the others in the group.

Carol said "You know Marie you can talk to me I would listen just like you do I feel better for talking to you about my family, we are friends aren't we Marie". "Yes we are Carol but my family is different to yours and anyway we are here to forget things for a while aren't we?"

Chapter Thirteen

Princess Anne

On some days we went to the beach and one day we visited a zoo where I saw James again but only in the distance. We were on the same coach on some outings and although we smiled and said hello we did not sit together. One day we had dinner early and were told to dress in these horrible stiff brownie uniforms, which were supplied for us. Then we went out to Sunshine Corner where we sang Jesus songs, we prayed a lot of thank yous, as we were very lucky to have places like this, so our parents could have a rest. I said to Carol "I bet my Mam and Dad were glad to be rid of us we're always falling out." I got a stern look from a woman at the end of the row. The Salvation Army man preached about Jesus, the story about the Sermon on the Mount, with the basket of fish and five loaves and how everyone got fed, and how grateful we all should be that we had full bellies and a roof over our heads and clothes on our bodies, then followed by a quote from the bible:

Matthew Ch 6 v 26 & 27 Look at the birds they do not sow seeds and yet their food is plentiful and why worry about clothes? Look at the wild flowers grow; they do not worry about clothes they are beautiful without having to make them, all these things come from Heaven.

The hall was very busy with lots of people in uniform. Then all at once the man said, "We have a special guest here tonight," then Princess Anne came onto the stage with a few other people. She spoke for a moment about the new centre, which we were standing in and Matron tapped me on the shoulder and asked me to come out from my seat. My first thoughts were what have I done now? I really thought I was in big trouble. I was trying to think what I had done, but she gave me a bunch of flowers and said take these to the stage and give them to Princess Anne when you are in front of her do the little curtsy which we have been practicing then you will line up for a photograph smile and do not fidget. I was so scared but did as I was told and a few others did the same. When I got to the stage, she bent down and said "Come up the steps." The six of us stood at the side of her and had our photograph taken just as Matron had said, I felt really good and I looked down to see Matron smiling at me then I spotted Betty smiling at me, then everyone stood up and we all sang the National Anthem and although I did not know the song at the time, it did seem quite a special song. When everything finished I saw James again. He had been in the hall with the boys all the time and I never noticed him. He must have seen me on the stage but he looked straight through me as if I was not there. I waved and he waved back so he must have seen me. Then I heard a man shout! "You get back in line boy." I just thanked God for James and hoped his camp was not as bad as it seemed. I said to Matron "That was so scary" she said "If I had told you beforehand you probably would not have done it, that's why we decided to choose when we arrived and you have practiced your curtsy lovely and that is why you were chosen." I smiled and said "Thank you."

The next morning at breakfast Betty said "Have you seen that brother of yours yet?" I smiled and said "He's okay just like you said, Betty, I was told this camp was horrid but I like it here, except I miss lots of things from home." Tears welled in my eyes as I thought of home; Betty said "I've heard yer Mam is in hospital?" I replied "I did not really know much, I know Mam has just had a baby." Betty looked at me, "She will be alright you're here so it makes it easier for your Dad that's all. Don't worry we do not want to keep you, other children will come after you go, I think two are arriving on Friday." I was so upset at the thought of home and I did miss baby June, instead of going walking, matron let me stay with Betty that day I said I had belly ache, so I lay on my bed for an hour then went to the kitchen to find Betty. She let me bake some cakes with her, I knew my way around the kitchen even at 9. Betty said "Well aren't you a little sur-

60

prise, do you cook at home?" I answered "Yes I have to do stuff for my brothers and look after my sisters, and help Mam as much as I can." "How many are there of you?" I said I had four brothers and a sister at that point. Betty smiled and said "Come on let's get on, the others will be back soon."

When the others came in for dinner, Betty said "Thank you Marie, go to your seat now," then she announced that I had made the crumble all by myself. Everyone clapped, Matron came over to me, "Well you feel better then, Marie?" "Yes matron I do." Matron said "Your mother is alright she's out of hospital and will be home when you return." "Thank you matron."

On the day we were leaving I gave Betty a hug she patted my shoulder and said things always work out Marie remember that. Then I said goodbye to matron. She gave me a smile "Be good you." Then I said bye to the others: some who were to stay another week and Carol who had become my best friend got on the bus with me and began to cry, which set me off crying. We agreed we would write to each other like pen pals we even exchanged address but we never did send any letters, I never got a letter or at least I don't think I did, Dad may have had mine so I suppose I could have but Dad would not have let me keep in touch. It was not worth the argument.

On the bus James was sat on his own he looked lost so I sat next to him and not next to Carol as I did when we came. All the way home he said very little about his stay at the holiday camp even though I chattered about my experience, he never ever wanted to talk about it, so I never brought the subject up again; all he said was he just hated it.

Mam was home when we got back but we could not hug her as she had a sore tummy where the stitches were. She had to rest a lot of the time, which meant I had to keep the young uns entertained, which I did anyway. Mam asked if we had a good time and whilst I replied yes I made some nice friends, James just left the room. He never spoke about it not then, not ever.

CHAPTER FOURTEEN

THE DOLLS HOUSE

I got out of bed to find the usual Christmas stocking hanging at the bottom of my bed and when I looked around the room I noticed the young uns had already gone downstairs. I do not know how they got past without waking me. I went to the bathroom and got dressed. I had a wash and cleaned my teeth with soot. Dad said he'd heard it was better than toothpaste and it was free; it never seemed to do us any harm and we all seem to have nice teeth so maybe that theory was right.

I went downstairs where the fire was blazing up the chimney and the smell of the turkey cooking. The television was on and the morning service was about the story of Jesus again which no one believed in except me. The nativity play was being acted out by a group of children at Southwell Minster. It was really good, with the choir singing Christmas carols. There was a massive tree in the corner of the church which made our tree look very small, but our tree was lovely because it was decorated with all our home made decorations. Mam always made sure we had pretty fairy lights on the tree as in the years gone by and they were always switched on ready for when we got up and although I still felt the disappointment from last Christmas I still loved it.

As I glanced around the room, there it was. My eyes lit up and filled with tears. I squealed with delight as I stood there staring at the dolls house the one I had dreamed of so many times. I had prayed for it so many times; Jesus, Mam and Dad had all answered last year's prayers, late but nevertheless answered. I was overwhelmed with emotions, my face was enough for Mam to break down into tears, and I hugged her and said, "Thank you". Mam & Dad both said "Thank you Marie" then Mam said "Marie you have been such a help to me today I do not want you to help me with the young UN's go and enjoy your dolls house."

The dolls house was exactly as I had imagined it; there was hardly anything in the dolls house, as Mam and Dad had saved up a long time for it. They explained I had no other gifts like the rest of them, I said this is fantastic I do not need anything else. I had made all my furniture and it would look great in my wonderful new dolls house. I ran upstairs to fetch it from my homemade cardboard house. Last year I said I was putting all the furniture in the bin but I did not have the heart to do so, as it took me many hours to make it. Instead I had made a dolls house out of cardboard boxes. I stacked them up in different sizes so I had two bedrooms, a kitchen and a sitting room. I was so glad I hadn't thrown away my furniture I had since began collected little toy people from jumble sales along with a dog and a horse.

The house was amazing the whole of the front including the roof opened up on hinges. It had windows in the part that opened then starting at the top there was an attic with a skylight window. It had two rooms: one painted yellow and the other orange my favour-ite colours. I said one would be the playroom and the orange room would be for James. He had always wanted a room of his own. There was a tiny train track in the attic room, which Dad had made from nails, and a tiny train, which he found at a jumble sale. The next floor had three bedrooms one had its very own bathroom, which was decorated in cream colours. That was Mam and Dad's room. Another bedroom was decorated in pink, which I said was my room. I had my very own wardrobe, which I had made and a few clothes, which Mam had sewn out of bits of cloth. The blue and green room was allocated to Robert, June and Carol. It had space for 3 beds and a wardrobe. Then there was another large bathroom, which stood alone; I had plans to tile it out of bits of tiles. It was magnificent and I wanted to tile it right away with mixed bright coloured mosaic tiles. They would be made from smashed up tiles that I had collected from the garden. I spotted them one day when Dad was digging so I sorted them out of the mud and washed them. It was like finding treasure in our very own garden, mainly blue and White with a few other colours, things like that excited me.

I had not thought about the bath, toilet and basin yet, I knew I wanted them all in white, but I had to wait until someone could show me how to make them. There was a winding staircase, which ran from the ground floor to the top floor, right up the middle of the house. It was a grand staircase with a handrail all the way up. I loved it.

On the ground floor there was a lounge, which had a large bay window. This was decorated in shades of brown and orange. I had made a TV, sofa, 2 chairs, a coffee table and a tall standard lamp. The dining room had cream painted walls and for this room I had made a table and six chairs and a sideboard to go along one wall. The kitchen was empty but would soon be fully fitted with all the tiny pots, pans, the smallest plates and cutlery I had ever seen, which Aunty had searched the country for; she gave these to me for my birthday, I was so happy. There were even tiny items of food, which James had made from Plasticine. There was another room, which I used to store all the spare furniture, which I was not using. I had lots of homemade furniture; I was able to change it all around to suit what mood I was in. All the windows had curtains, which Mam made for me and all the rooms had fitted carpets, which Dad had put in for me from bits people gave him because we didn't have fitted carpets in our own house only lino and bare boards.

There was a garage attached to the back of the house, James gave me one of his toy cars, which fitted in the garage perfect. I also made a small stable out of one of the Christmas boxes, for Ned my toy horse. Oh this was so special I couldn't believe my eyes.

It was perfect just perfect, I cried with excitement I just could not believe I owned my very own dollhouse.

James liked to play with the house too. He made fences out of lolly sticks and trees from cotton wool and twigs from the garden outside.

The best furniture was the home made from odds and ends. Over time I would have a family of little wooden figures and I would imagine some of the figures were friends and family. There was a dog -called Scruff and a cat called Tipsy and I even had a horse, which James gave me from an old farmyard set. James named the horse Ned. We even made a pond from tin foil for the garden. The house was truly amazing, and well used, every spare moment I would be in my bedroom playing with my dolls house or making things to put inside. I was truly happy and could not stop looking at it. I was always rearranging the furniture and thanking God for answering my prayer.

We, I mean I, was expecting John any day now but he did not show up. I asked Dad where he was and he said we have no room and he is staying at your auntie's but he will come on Christmas Day. Again I did not understand, as there was a single bed empty in George's room, I tried to ask but was told it was none of my business, but it was. He was my brother too. James said Dad had fallen out with him and the aunt who he was now living with. I was upset but I got used to disappointments in my life. He did come to see us and gave me a big hug. I told him all about the dolls house and took him to see it. We sat and talked for ages as we had lots to say to each other. He asked me how the family was coping and if James and I still argued? I just said it's what brothers and sisters do, it's accepted. I told him about Dad hitting James on a regular basis and he said that's why he might not come home to stay again. He also said things had not been right between him and Dad for a while. I cried and said, "Please we miss you, and I miss you." He said we would still write to each other. John never came home to stay ever again. Dad blamed the aunt who ran the pub and fell out with her forever in a massive bust up, but really Dad had driven him away with all the drunkenness, shouting, accusations and beatings.

CHAPTER FIFTEEN

WHOOPING COUGH

Carol was coming up to a year old and developed whooping cough. She was very ill all through the night, with a high temperature and a terrible cough. The next day an ambulance came and took her to hospital where she stayed for one whole week and for her 1st birthday we had a party in her absence. The aunties came and the drinks cabinet was opened once again. It was a Sunday, and Carol's Godmother came over from Leicester. There were lots of nice things to eat: jelly, cake, sandwiches and juice, also alcohol for the adults, we had a nice day. I had a black eye and a swollen cheek from something that had happened at school. Some of us at school were running around the desks when I fell and banged my face smack on the upper cheekbone. The schoolteacher took me to hospital to check for concussion but I was okay, the doctor said I would probably have a shiny black eye, which came a few days later so there was no dispute as to how that had happened it did hurt but not for too long.

Carol was given the all clear from the hospital and she was out of danger. She was allowed home 2 days after her 1st birthday she missed all the fun but was only a baby so did not know what it was about anyway.

George was bringing home girlfriends and whilst they did not do any harm to us they were not really very nice to us either. Why was everyone nasty I would ask, but no logical answer was given? Music played from a record player, which was a long sideboard type brown wooden cabinet, a real piece of furniture. The Rolling Stones, Elvis, and The Beatles were in the pop charts but the Hollies, Donovan and Bob Dylan played non-stop in our house my eldest brother and his girlfriends listened to it constantly. I just went to my room out of the way, otherwise he said "fetch this, fetch that." I spent a lot of time in my room in the evenings; I was better out of the way. It did not stop them shouting me down to make a pot of tea or to make some toast and jam. As soon as I gave them what they wanted they shouted, "Well go on then, you're not stopping here." It wasn't as though I really wanted to be with them slopping over each other whilst he and the girl ate sweets or chocolates which they never once offered out to anyone else. So the other kids and I stayed in my room where we often made dens within the bunk beds. The room was a total mess by the time we had done and we often slept all night in the dens we built that day, it was me who had to tidy up after so it did not really matter.

One day I heard in the news Martin Luther King say in a speech in Washington that he dreamt and prayed that the sons of slaves would be able to sit down together in harmony, and bury the differences of their forefathers. I thought about that very hard at the time and could not come to any understanding. I began to wonder whether I was a slave and what about my father? One politician or another said sometimes things on the news, which never made any sense, but I supposed the adults understood.

About the same time the vicar said in a story "The lambs will graze with the lions" and another time he said, "The children will bear the sins of their forefathers" though I didn't understand any of it I always remembered the words.

CHAPTER SIXTEEN

OBSESSED

In 1964 we had moved into the big bedroom, George had left home to live in a flat. I shared my room with June and Carol and the small room was now the bedroom of James and Robert.

We had bunk beds in both rooms but I had my own single bed and had put posters on my walls of horses and pop groups; this was my piece of wall so I covered it. My dolls house stood proud on a table next to my bed. My perfect family lived in the house. Some had the same names as my real family, little figures painted in colours to suit male or female. The dolls house was a big part of my childhood life, a special gift given to me, which I had many happy hours rearranging. I pretended this was a perfect make believe family. I made new furniture, each piece better than the last. I even made a garden, which ran around the outside of the big house. This was the dolls house I had prayed for and dreamt of owning for almost two years, now it was mine at last, given to me for Christmas from Mam and Dad via Santa and God.

I was almost obsessed with the dolls house, where my ideal make-believe family lived. I became withdrawn, and quiet, spending hours rearranging the rooms, making sure my make-believe family were positioned right. If any figures fell over I would pick them up and talk to them as if I knew them personally. My ideal family usually got on without arguments and beatings. There was harmony and peace in my dolls house and my mind felt at peace with my make-believe family.

Dad said it was abnormal behaviour and I heard Mam saying to Dad it was my age. I would grow out of it. But they did not understand the secret that I held dominated my mind it was hidden deep within me, tormenting me. It was as if it was eating my inside away, making me feel hollow and limp. I felt like my emotions were breaking down and my thoughts were evolving into bad thoughts. I felt that my life was nothing. I was worth nothing. Mam tried to make more time for James and me because we began hating each other verbally. Although he was abused physically, his emotions came out in the form of aggression towards the rest of us. Because he never knew about my abuse, instead of embracing each other through our torment, we argued more and more. He was the one who was hard done to; he thought I was always, Goody Two shoes, butter would not melt, in his mind. So I just agreed with him because he was abused and he suffered inside too, I knew that. We just did not get on anymore, not at all. We were being driven apart by simply growing up and both being abused in different ways. Why couldn't our parents see how we were changing? Why couldn't they understand the wrongdoing to the both of us?

When I was not in my room playing with the dolls house or making furniture for it, Dad would call me to his room. It was usually when the house was empty but sometimes he called me when other people were downstairs, he was getting more daring. My brothers and sisters would all say I was Dad's favourite. Why didn't anyone ask why he wanted me to go to him? Mam even said, "Go on then he's asking for you." Surely Mam knew. Why didn't she stop him? She was equally to blame for everything that happened to my brother and I, maybe she was just as scared as we were I could never understand and will never know the answer.

I know I was his first-born girl and did get more attention than any of my brothers or sisters. He spoilt me too. He would take me to the pub on a Sunday lunch, "Put on your best dress Marie." He would say to his mates "This is my daughter", he was so proud to have me with him. "Isn't she lovely," he would say? "She is the best daughter any Dad could have, she cleans and cooks and does everything a little woman should do." Then he would parade me around like some sort of trophy. Mam never liked him taking me to the pub, and she would shout down the path "Leave her here!" But Dad would take

me by the hand and drag me down the street. He bought me chocolate and drinks, and gave me coppers and said, "Don't tell the others
I have treated you." Then when we got home after he had his dinner,
he would call me into his room, for a so-called nap, or at least that's
what he told the others anyway. It was nearly always after he had
been drinking and this happened on a regular basis that I would lay
next to my Dad, who I loved, in fear.

I wrote to John often and sometimes contemplated telling him my
secret. I would fill him in on what was happening at home, and
school, but although I thought about it I never actually wrote my
entire secret down. Oh I was so close to it. I even began a sentence,
but could never quite finish it. I tore it into little pieces in case anyone should piece it together. I even remember burning one letter,
where I know I wrote too much about what was happening to us. I
threw it on the fire; just too scared of the consequences.

I still loved my dolls house and looked at it every day. I dusted it
occasionally but did not give it the attention it deserved. I became
more and more withdrawn losing interest in playing with anything
or anybody. I never did much at all really. I would do my homework
from school and all the jobs in the house for Mam, but did not feel
like playing or mixing with others. I had June and Carol who felt
like my own children and I was very protective of them where Dad
was concerned.

I felt I was an uninteresting and not a very pretty girl my hair was
dull with no style and to add to my misery I started to gain weight,
I felt no emotions and had no aim in life. I had no need for friends
because I never went out unless I went to Linda's house, which was
not very often. Her Mam did not like me and she thought I was a
bad influence on her daughter. I don't know why she felt that way
I think it was because I was from a big family and just was not
good enough for her. I felt like a failure no matter what I did I was
wrong where my brothers were concerned. My confidence was being shattered and battered out of me; to some extent this followed
me throughout my adult life until my healing began and even now
although confident in most things I fail at others and although I
rarely dwell on the past anymore on occasion something crops up to
remind me.

CHAPTER SEVENTEEN

SPAIN

Aunt Bess went to Spain every year with my Uncle and this year she asked Mam if I could go with them, when Mam said yes I just could not believe it. Aunt Bess paid for everything she even made all the cotton dresses for the holiday. Mam bought new sandals, socks and pants and a nice swimsuit, different from the navy school one it was a soft turquoise with small white flowers printed all over it, Mam knitted a lovely white cardigan to take, I was so excited by this wonderful adventure and opportunity to go on an aeroplane to fly across the ocean.

We arrived at the airport with our cases it was very busy with people everywhere with luggage on trolleys, we checked in and went through to the departure lounge where we awaited instruction to board the plane. I remember being nervous to the point of shaking not sure whether it was nerves or excitement, we found our place and sat in a row of three my Uncle being near the window. I was in the middle and Aunt Bess was in the aisle seat, the plane took off my ears went pop, pop and the pain was excruciating the air hostess gave me some sweets to suck hoping they would help, which they did, then all at once the pilot asked everyone to take their seats the plane began to rock from side to side it was like being at the Goose Fair which is held in Nottingham on the Forest every year.

Then the plane dropped, like dropping from the sky I could hear people being sick, I was petrified and felt I was going to be sick but managed to hold it down all the people I could see had a brown bag in their hand, some girls in the seats behind us were actually screaming, my Uncle asked them to shut up as they were becoming a little hysterical. The pilot spoke to everyone saying we were in a bad thunderstorm to stay calm and that he was sorry he had to drop to avoid the storm and hoped everyone was all right, people began to calm down and the flight carried on with no more drama.

We arrived at the Hotel late at night to find it was double booked and we had to move to another Hotel, which was another 30 minutes away and was a nicer one. Aunt Bess and Uncle had a double room but there was no bed for me. I was a young girl who slept in a room on my own at least for one night then the next day the Hotel manager said they had no spare rooms and that I was too young to sleep alone, so the manager asked my Aunt if I could stay with another woman a complete stranger who was on her own in a twin bedded room, she had agreed.

The woman's name was Adele she was 28 years old I was just 13. Adele was French and spoke fairly good English and said it would be good for her to converse with me, she was really nice, and she wore wonderful clothes very glamorous she put her makeup on me in the evening and allowed me to wear her beautiful smelling perfume, this could never happen today my Aunt trusted her, I never knew what she did for a job accept she did have 4 weeks in Spain which led me to believe she was a school teacher she kind of acted the type if you know what I mean.

I awoke one morning to find the wall was black with beetles I cried I cannot be in this room they were in my bed I ran outside to find the pathway to the main Hotel was covered in cockroaches the storm the previous night had brought everything to life as Spain had not had any rain for months, Adele went crazy and demanded the room was fumigated immediately, the rooms were single storey a little like wooden huts in a row and all around were beautiful gardens with tennis courts to one side, and a kidney shaped pool with sun terraces, I had to repack all my clothes then unpack them again but not before Adele examined every corner of the room including the wardrobe and beds.

Adele was on the beach from 10 am until the sun went down she was a real sun worshipper, she was brown all over as she sunbathed topless with a tiny triangle of a bikini bottom. She never lay near us; she preferred to be alone after all she was really with us.

I often went into the sea for a paddle or swim without Aunt Bess although I have never been brave in the sea, if anything I am somewhat nervous for fear of what lurks beneath but the sea was clear so clear you could see the bed of pale beige sand beneath your feet, there was no seaweed in this part of the sea and it was lovely and warm as the sun was very hot, one day I was swimming in my depth a little way out when I looked back to the beach it was like looking at something from a film, a whirlwind shot across the beach destroying everything in its path, the parasols, towels and sun loungers were flying everywhere someone shouted to those of us in the sea stay where you are you are safer, I was scanning the beach for Aunt Bess but the whole beach looked different the sand was swirling around and it was hard to focus, it was horrific the shop front canopies were being torn off, people did not know which way to run there had not been any warning, the storm only lasted a matter of minutes but the debris looked like a war had just taken place. Aunt Bess and Uncle came to fetch me as I stood frozen in the sea with not much thought other than I was going to die if the whirlwind came my way into the sea, I could not move with the fear, they shouted me to come out, I suddenly came back to reality, they wrapped a towel around me and took me for a drink and I calmed down with the thoughts in my head that I was stranded in a foreign country without anyone if it killed my Auntie and Uncle.

It was quite amazing shop keepers and café' waiters and people passing by was running around

Tidying up putting parasols back, sorting out shop canopies and any debris flying around, it seamed that no-one was really injured the police was there in seconds along with ambulances everyone pulling together the cafés' were giving out free drinks to calm peoples fears and all of a sudden the wind was gone the heat was unbearable and everyone went back to the beach tidying as they went, almost as if nothing had happened within the hour people were laying back on the beach.

Aunt Bess said "Well you have had all your experiences in one week what a holiday you have had, I wonder if you will venture to Spain again?" "Yes a few memories to hold onto there Aunt Bess".

I said my goodbyes to Adele and we promised to write, which I did for years, Adele wrote back on occasion and sent gifts from France just small things but they meant such a lot to me, all the mail went to Aunties so I got it that time. I kept in touch with Adele for many years exchanging gifts and cards Dad said it was unnatural for a women her age to want to keep in touch with a girl so I told him I had stopped just to keep the peace, I carried on for a while but then I heard nothing ever again just lost contact, my memory of her would be her complete kindness to me and true friendship it could have been so different had I been older. No one had asked about my holiday when I got home, Mam just said did you have a nice time no detail was asked for, so no details were given. It's funny really I thought things would have changed while I was away but I went home to the same.

CHAPTER EIGHTEEN

MY DAY DREAM

As I lay there wishing my life could be different I found myself staring at the dolls house. My perfect family came to life right before my eyes sending me into a trancelike state, a daydream.

"Marie what are you doing?" "I am doing my home-work Mam." "Is your brother helping you, it is always better that you help each other?" "Yes Mam he is here, we are okay thanks Mam." Dad knocked on the door, "Hello you two what are you up to, can I help in any way?" James said "Yes Dad we would like that, this is the perfect subject for you as Marie is doing a project at school on coal mines, when coal mining began and how it is formed in the earth."

Dad said "I have just the book which will answer all your questions Marie I will go and fetch it for you." He came back with a plate of home made cakes and some drinks on a tray. "There you go one book and Mam has sent these to keep you going until dinner is ready. We are having steak pie today with Daddy's home grown cabbage and carrots." "Umm yummy" we both replied together. "What's for pudding, jam sponge and custard?" "How did you guess?" James giggled, "Well the sponge cakes were a bit of a giveaway." Dad said "Mam has been baking all afternoon, don't forget to thank her after dinner, I must say it's very warm in here, is it this warm in your room James? I always worry with you being in the attic." "Yes Dad it's great I love my room." "I will shout you when dinner is ready. After dinner we can go to the park with Robert and the dog and maybe we could have a kick about with that new football of yours James." James smiled and said "Yes Dad I would like that perhaps you could show me how to head the ball. It always seems to end up in my face and it's pain-

ful." "Can we go to Wollaton Park in the car Dad?" "No, we will walk to the local park because it will be too late and Wollaton Park closes its gates and we will be trapped inside all night with the ghosts." Dad bent down and tickled us both until we collapsed in a heap together on the floor. We all laughed loudly and Dad left us to eat the cakes and finish my homework. James said "Marie do you believe in ghosts, I do?" "I'm not sure, I have never seen one but there must be ghosts because the vicar talks about the Holy Ghost quite often in church. I suppose they must be real because why would he say it after all he is a vicar so he should not tell lies to us should he?" James replied, "I don't know about that I do not understand what he is talking about half the time, except the Jesus bit."

James picked up the book and looked up in the index about coal, which was what we needed to help with the project, and I scribbled it down rough in pencil. Then I would copy it out in pen in my best handwriting another day as I had two weeks to finish the project.

In my dream state, my bedroom was lovely with cream wallpaper and pink flowers, which seemed to cascade from the ceiling into the cream carpet. I had a pink flowery bedspread with pure white cotton sheets and a lavender blanket on my bed. James and I sat at the desk on two chairs, which were just the right height; the desk had a flip top lid with an ink well sunk into the top right hand corner. The lid opened into a hiding place for my schoolbooks. I allowed James to use my desk to do his homework when he wanted, as he did not have a table in his room. We were always happy to help each other and shared similar interests. The cat lay asleep on the padded chair which I used to put my clothes on until Mam came and sorted them for the wash or hung them up in the wardrobe which was made of light coloured wood. I also had a small table at the side of my bed where a lamp stood with a delicate pink shade on it with tassels, which hung like threads of silk. The curtains matched my bedspread; behind them were lacy white nets, which hung in an arch so I could see outside, through the large panes of glass. On my windowsill I had collected all sorts of trinket boxes in wood, glass and plastic all different shapes and colours the glass shone in the sunlight.

We finished the homework and James said "I will thrash you at snakes and ladders without cheating." He gave me a gentle push and said "Well shall

I fetch it from my room or not?" I said "Okay but you will not win you know I am the champion when you do not cheat." He ran off laughing and I sat chuckling to myself and thinking how much I loved my life.

Mam came in for the tray and kissed me on my head and I asked her why my friend's Mam had died. She said, "Well illness sometimes takes over the body and it does not get better, like the budgie we had. Do you remember when we took it to the vet? He said it had a growth and that it was the budgie's time to die. If you think about it, all life always comes to an end after a time, as we cannot live forever, otherwise we would be overcrowded. We have very little control over our time on earth; it is God's decision when our time is up. Even flowers, trees and insects only have a certain time to live and they get diseases just as we do. I know it's hard to understand at your age especially when you see people like grandma living to be very old. Then you hear of someone young dying but I'm afraid death is part of life if that makes sense." "But will you die Mam?" "No not yet I'm not going anywhere. I want to see my grandchildren, now that's enough of that talk." "I love you Mam." James was taught to knock on the door like Dad did just in case I was getting changed or something. But this time he knew I was waiting for him so he burst in with the snakes and ladders game. Mam said "I love you both very much, hugged us both and said laughing "I bags you the red disc, I'll just have time for one game before I see to dinner and no cheating James." We all enjoyed our game though James always managed to cheat and win. We all laughed and hugged, but it was only a game just like my daydream a game of make-believe with my perfect family, in my beautiful dolls house.

CHAPTER NINETEEN

THE MINES

There were thousands of men who worked down the mines all over the British Isles. It was our industry; coal kept us warm, paid the wages and gave generations of boys and men work through two World Wars. The miners were often working to rule or only working a three-day week as the coal seams became less productive and efficient in the 1970s. Sometimes for the better but often not, it was the men and their families who suffered the sheer frustration of having no money, no warmth, no food and no jobs in some cases. The rows and anger contributed to times of family war. They broke under the pressure of their home life then they had the pressure of work colleagues. The country was in turmoil and it seemed everyone blamed the miners for the trouble. They were greedy and that was that. It was the miners' fault the country was going to the dogs, but they did do a harrowing job. Down under the ground miles and miles of seams and shafts were dug out so the men could dig for the precious coal which generated millions of pounds worth of revenue and helped the economy. We all took them for granted, working in thick dense wet soot with only a helmet torch for vision. They urinated where they stood and ate their food sitting on the floor or a heap of debris. The mine would sometimes collapse under pressure and throughout the years hundreds of men lost their lives or were maimed. In later years many hundreds of miners would be diagnosed with chronic emphysema. Yes, it was very hard for the miners but the Government was not going to give in. Both sides were too stubborn to give in so the pain was created.

This was the sixties and seventies when life was beginning to look better for British Industry. Then it got worse for the miners in the seventies, when Ted Heath was in power, but the sixties were good in many ways: the Beatles, Rolling Stones and Elvis the King were all singing to everyone through radios and televisions, which were now in every household and telephones were also becoming popular. If you worked hard life could only get better. There was the contraceptive pill and free love and of course drugs were rife. Young people had a ball growing up in the rock and roll era.

It was winter when the miners went on a three-day week. The schools and factories closed after a while because there was no fuel for the heating. The street lights were not lit because it was coal that generated the power stations and the coal was not being delivered so it ran out. There was an element of excitement in our house for the children as we all went around scaring each other in the dark, or at least in the beginning. Money was short but Dad still managed to find the money to go to the pub and in our house the shouting got louder between the adults. Mam cried a lot more and Dad got more aggressive towards my brothers.

It was dark as I walked home. I noticed the glistening ice was already forming on the pavements showing it was to be a very cold night. I walked through the house. I noticed no fire was lit and the back door was wide open. I looked out the door and saw Dad, and shouted, "Do you want a cup of tea Dad?" I walked back into the kitchen to fill the kettle and I heard my brother shout, "There is no electricity you bloody fool." "Well isn't there any gas either? I can put a saucepan on." I received no answer so I went back to the door. Dad was standing at the back step chopping wood for the fire. Dad looked up at me in horror and dismay. I could only just make out his features and that look of horror on his face in the dark. He said "You're too old for this now, and you do not play with it anymore."

I did a double take. I did not recognise all the bits of wood lying in a pile on and around the step. I said "What are you doing Dad?" Dad just stared at me. I could not identify or connect the wood on the ground as being my beautiful dolls house. It was the look he gave me that made me realise what he had just said and he stared into my face without any expression. I ran to my room to find an empty table beside my bed. The anger was welling up inside, why, why? I ran into Mam's bedroom and screamed "Where is she, where is me Mam?" "Mam's not in," Robert shouted. I do not think this would have happened if Mam were home. "Dad where is Mam?" I opened the landing window and shouted "Dad where's Mam?" Dad did not look up but he said, "She's in hospital, she was taken in this morning, she is not well again and the coal has not come. The house was too cold and we needed some firewood." He then carried on sweeping together my precious dolls house. The bits had flown off in every direction, he had emptied the furniture on the bed but what use was that now? I looked at it and threw it all into a corner with a sweep of my arm, sending some of it on to the lino, like discarded junk, the furniture which I had put together with my own hands. I had collected all the bits of wood and fabric, anything that could be transformed into furniture.

Suddenly the darkness became completely black with no streetlights it was darker than usual. Later when the fire was lit with my dolls house it lit up the room for a while, but the wood only burnt for a short while, I carried some of the furniture downstairs and threw it to the back of the fire grate. I said "There, you might as well have the lot, are you nice and warm Dad, are you?" The sparks flew around and up the chimney. Dad said, "You didn't have to do that, you could have used boxes for the house like before, you are clever and imaginative with that sort of thing, you made your cardboard house look really good; you could have made do again. I have chopped up the piano up, as well it was not just the dolls house, no one ever played on that piano. It just sat there with a vase of plastic flowers on it collecting dust." I could not argue with that I thought. "Marie I needed to do it, we have to keep warm, I made a pan of stew earlier we'll have some soon." I could not believe he was carrying on as if nothing had happened and the thought of eating his stew made me want to vomit. "I hate you," I mumbled. Dad stood up "What did you say?" I ran to the door and shouted, "I hate you, I really hate you." The tears flooded down my face as I ran to my room.

I wiped the tears from my eyes and threw myself on the bed still shouting with rage and hate in complete darkness, my hatred was frightening, I honestly thought of killing myself that night because I also hated what I was saying and doing but I didn't know how. Even worse than wanting to kill myself I started thinking about killing my own Dad because of the hate I felt for him. The thing I loved more than anything in the whole world was gone in a puff of smoke for ten minutes warmth at the most. I stared at the empty table where my perfect dolls house once stood with my perfect family who never argued. I tried to focus on the table beside me and noticed the animals still in place, the horse from James' farmyard set and the pond shining as it was made of foil with a duck in the middle and the reeds still standing there. I cried some more, with my rib cage aching I felt my life was coming to an end, Mam was ill, my brother James was always out or beating me up when he was in, my brother John was away in the Navy, George did not live with us anymore and did not care anyway. All that was left was three youngsters me, and a brother, and with a Dad who was abusing me at any given opportunity. Where was God now come on God where are you? Show me where you are now? How could I end my misery my very unhappy life?

As I lay on my bed I began to think back to when I asked Santa if toys were taken off children if they were bad. I remembered what he said Why no once he gave them they was ours to keep, I also remembered I had a beautiful dolls pram, which was built the same as a real baby's coach pram only on a smaller scale. It had pink satin covers and a baby doll that looked so real. I loved that too, it was a Christmas gift but before January was out, it was gone. Another year I had a big doll, which stood two feet tall, it walked and talked and had long blonde hair. Mam won it at the bingo that too disappeared. As children we never knew where our toys went we just knew that they left the house after Christmas. James and I each had a bike, we rode them every day after school but they were sold after about 3 months, Dad sold them and said we were too rough with them because we often had punctured tyres.

I wrote to John to ask him if he thought I was a bad girl. I wanted to know why people at school didn't like me and why I was bullied. I also asked him why we were given gifts only for them to be taken away. It was so cruel to let us have nice things only to take them away weeks later. It would have been better not to have them in the first place. Oh the neighbours were impressed, with the posh gifts we were having these days but James and I were devastated by it so much so that we did not look forward to gifts anymore as we knew they would disappear and this haunted us for years to come it was like mind games playing with our emotions. Mam and Dad had no idea of the harm they were doing to us mentally.

Dad interrupted my thoughts and said, "I know what will make you feel better, and let's have a cuddle? The others are happy downstairs eating their stew." I pretended to be asleep, with anxiety and dread filling my thoughts, he touched me and I squirmed away from the hand that touched my arm. I smelt his putrid cigarette breath on my neck. He pulled me off the bed quite hard so I banged my head on the table. He said "I know you are not asleep, come on, come with me I will make you feel better, I feel really bad about chopping up that doll's house, so will you comfort me?" He tugged my arm. I had no choice but to go to his room. Again the warning came from his mouth directly into my ear, but the invitation could not be refused.

Chapter Twenty

Daddy's Little Girl

Mam's illness was gradual over five years. She had some good days, some bad days, some very bad days and she was in and out of hospital for the whole five years. It was very hard on the family and me. James and I were growing up. I had to take care of my three youngest siblings who were three, four and seven. I overheard Mam saying to a neighbour that she had been diagnosed with cancer shortly after Carol was born. That's why we all went away for two weeks in the summer. Of course I did not know what cancer was, and never paid any attention to what I had heard because as far as I was concerned it was adult business anyway.

Dad was paying more and more attention to me. The week after the dolls house was chopped up for firewood Dad beat James to a pulp, which none of the others could ever understand? Mam was not in at the time she was never in when he hit him and just like me, James kept it quiet.

The curtains had been drawn together and the door was locked behind us. The door had a small lock, which slid across. I lay there next to him as usual, usually it was a cuddle and just a touch of his thing on top of his trousers, and he would say this is our special time together. His hand took hold of my hand as he led it across his stomach, on top of his trousers. "Marie I know you are upset about the dolls house but we'll make it better, you might even get a better one someday, if you are a good girl to Daddy because you are Daddy's little girl aren't you?" I tried to pull back and he gripped it tight and moved it down further onto his bulge. He said, "Touch it, it won't hurt you, tickle me like you tickle the girls. I love to watch you make them laugh, they love you so much just like I do." I was so frightened; *this is my Dad, is this what I'm supposed to do?* Then he said "Put your hand inside Marie just this once." He unzipped his trousers and guided my hand inside on top of his underpants but then he pushed my hand into the slit. I could feel hair and then he pushed my hand to his bulge and said "Touch it Marie, tickle it, they're only soft balls, with skin on them they won't hurt you." His hand lay firm on my wrist so I could not pull away. Then his thing grew longer, and went very hard. I snapped my hand away in fear; it was not this bad on top of his trousers. I gulped hard as he said grip it hard, don't be scared. I had no idea what this all meant of course. I was so scared then he forced my hand up and down his thing inside his underpants, with his hand tight over mine so I could not pull away and I dare not disobey. Then the warning came again: "This is our secret." Then he moaned sending sticky stuff all over his stomach, with just a little bit going on my hand. It was horrible, I felt sick and my stomach was in knots. I was silent and motionless my heart was racing with fear of what was next. Then he said as calm as can be with no emotion, "Go now and pass me some toilet paper there's a good girl, and there is a bar of chocolate in my trouser pocket, and don't forget you're my girl. This is our secret you do not tell a soul. Do you hear me?"

This had been worse than the times before, I had not had any contact with a man's flesh before, I still hadn't seen it because it was dark, but now I had touched it, I thought it was repulsive.

Mam was so ill she couldn't go to him, so I was sent to him often, I did as I was told without question. Nobody knew the emotional pain I was going through. I suffered alone, completely alone; neither God nor human could stop these atrocities over which I had no control.

I went back to Sunday school. I needed something where I was out of the house, but Dad soon put a stop to it. He said I was Church of England and why was I going to the Evangelical church, but I went on Thursday nights anyway disobeying him. I went to the church club and just said I was at a friend's house, Mam knew but said, "Don't tell yer Dad."

I got to know some of the helpers one who was a Sunday school teacher. She was really nice, but she sometimes probed questions at me so I began to open up to her about a few little things.

Not my secret though. She was very calm and Godly and looking back I think she knew things were not right at home. I never told her of my secret though I was close a couple of times but dare not, my Dad had warned me. I might have told her more given time but Dad interfered. The lady used to give me a lift home most weeks but I had to stop going because Mam said Dad suspected, as it was a regular thing. Then one night out of the blue the Sunday school teacher knocked on the door because I had not been to the club for two weeks. She thought I was ill, and said she had missed me at the club. When Dad answered the door he went crazy with the lady and told her not to be nosey and not to interfere with family business, and to clear off. The fact he knew nothing of the club made him very cross he also feared me getting too close to any adults in case I told them anything. Dad said "Marie is not coming to the damn church anymore so leave her alone."

I was never able to go back, I did not dare disobey him again; Mam went mad at me because Dad found out and Mam got shouted at. In turn she shouted at me saying "You do as you are told you're not going anymore. Who was that woman anyway?" I told Mam she was a very kind Sunday school teacher. I heard some months later she had died of cancer, which made me cry, as I liked her. I asked Mam what cancer was but she looked away and never answered me.

Chapter Twenty One

The Park

We had two parks within walking distance of our house, one we called the bottom park. This was about ten minutes walk but took us twenty minutes to walk it at our pace of walking, bearing in mind I always had a pram and two or three young uns in tow. We passed two blocks of shops and some of the shopkeepers knew the whole family. Because of the fact that I would run down to the shops in school lunchtime for Mam, they got to know me very well. There was one shop, which was run by a very old lady, this was a shop like Aladdin's cave. She always waved to me from when I went in for odds and ends and also knew me from church. There was also a greengrocer where I bought the potatoes, a newsagent where I got Mam's magazines from and the launderette where later I would go on a Monday to do loads and loads of washing. In the second block of shops under the bridge there was a hairdresser, bookies, my favourite sweet shop, a nice butcher, a grocers and a post office. I never liked the people in there because they accused our family of stealing sweets so I avoided that place like the plague. On the other side of the road there was the wood yard. It was very loud with a lot of big machinery, giant saws and lifting equipment that was used to fill the big lorries with the trees that appeared to be 60 yards long taller than a house but they laid on the ground and must they have been a yard wide. I knew all this because I was fascinated and would take a detour to the entrance to watch the men doing their work. I even asked for a small log or two for the fire and they gave it to me willingly. Then they would say, "Now go away you kids you should not be here it is too dangerous." I would put the logs into the tray underneath the pram and shout "Bye and thanks see you again another day." They would wave and shout back.

At the back of the park was a wood with some very old trees and shrubbery in it and old walls and a stream. I was told it was previously a pig farm some years ago. Through the woods there was a meadow full of long grass, yellow buttercups and daisies. I loved to go there, it even had a stream running through it, I found great pleasure in taking my brother and two sisters there, and it was like a peaceful paradise. We sometimes took fishing nets and on nice spring days we would fish for frogs and lift the spawn out with our hands. It slid through our fingers like snot from a runny nose with the bogies attached which of course were the tadpoles at the earliest stage of life. We would scream with laughter as it slithered back into the water and drifted away with the small current of the stream. Sometimes we managed to capture a little bit of it and put it into jam jars with a little weed. We carefully took it home, in the bottom of the pram trying not to slop the water onto the baby blanket. When we got home we transferred it into a bucket or bowl, added a few stones and more water and over the days watched the spawn turn into tadpoles and then into tiny frogs. Then we let them go in the garden. The park area had a set of four swings, and another set of three baby swings, a very tall slide, a spider's web roundabout and a low to the ground a spinning top roundabout. With the trees to climb there was plenty to occupy us for the whole day. There were always lots of other children either playing football or who had a skipping rope, which we could play with, as they were fairly friendly. Most of the other children were with their parents. If we made friends with the children the parents would invite us to join in the picnic, which they brought with them. Sometimes we said yes and tucked into sandwiches and cake, until the mothers began asking questions like where do you come from then? Where is your Mam? How come you have the baby? I was only asked because I was only about ten or eleven myself. As soon as the questions started I was off, being warned by Dad "You never tell anyone our business, they are all nosey beggars, you tell them nothing."

The other park was on Toll Lane, approximately 10 minutes away, across the busy main road. This park was not as good as the other one and we did not pass a shop on the way unless we walked to the bottom of the hill to a grocer's shop. There the sweets were in packets, which were too expensive as we only ever had a few pennies. They also had separate boxes, which you could mix, but only one or two jellies or liquorice for one penny. We never had enough money to buy the packets and the others were gone before we reached the park. The people in this shop were grumpy and did not like children going in the shop. They watched us as we chose what we wanted and sometimes said, "Do you have any money?" as we entered the shop. We chose this park by way of a change but only when we had no money and we were often bored by lunchtime.

The park had two sides to it and we called it the top park. It had a large playing field surrounded by railings. We were not allowed to go on that grass but there was other grass in kind of humps, which was fun to roll down until we landed in some dog poo. Then we called each other stinky for the rest of the day. Dogs were not restricted in those days, so they messed anywhere. There was a winding path in between the play areas and we played there if we had a ball. There was also a pavilion where the footballers would get changed, ready for their football match. There were some toilets, which were smelly and covered in graffiti and a hut where a park keeper would sit. He would come out on occasion and tell us off if we were not behaving. He shouted "Hey what you doing? You can't do that," or "Get off there you can't go on there." Our play was limited to the swings and the roundabout, sometimes we would run to the bottom park where there was more to dog frame; we liked the bottom park because the park keeper hardly ever came there.

The park at the bottom had sets of six swings, with two baby swings on each. There was a tall slide and a shorter slide; a bobby's helmet roundabout and a wooden spider's web with bars going to the middle in bright colours. We used to get chalky pieces of stone from a rockery on the corner of the park, which were in different colours. We lay down on the roundabout, hung onto a rail and drew circles all around it with the other hand. We often caught our knuckles and made them bleed whilst we took it in turns to scooter it to make it spin fast.

There was one time when I was more than grateful for the grumpy park keeper. June was three years old and enjoyed chalking like us whilst the roundabout was spinning slowly, but whilst I was watching Robert come down the slide, she climbed on the roundabout. Another lad spun it around and around. She was trying to hold on but one of her legs fell to the tarmac and got dragged underneath. It was completely wedged underneath, she was screaming and crying. We all ran over including the park keeper who just happened to be around thank goodness on that occasion. He rang the ambulance then the fire brigade. I was upset and Robert was crying. June's leg was so tight under the wood the fire brigade had to dismantle the platform of the roundabout. Then the police came asking questions including where is your mother? I told them she had gone shopping in Bulwell so he put a call out. Where is your Dad? He's at work. Can you get in your house? I said "Yes Mam never locked the door, but what about June?" He said that an ambulance was taking her to hospital. Then I started crying so the policewoman said "Not to worry, she'll be alright but you need to go home in case your Mam comes home." I put Robert on the pram Carol was sat up oblivious and off I went crying all the way. The policeman walked with us as far as the main road to ensure we got across safely even though we had crossed it hundreds of times before. He then went his own way.

Later a policeman came to the house with Mam in the car and I explained what had happened. Mam did not get cross with me, like I thought she would, she just told me to put the shopping away, take care of the children and asked me to give them something to eat. She said she would be ages at the hospital. Then she left with the policeman shouting back at me "Tell your Dad when he gets home."

I made beans on toast for us and gave Carol a small piece of toast followed by a bottle made with Rusk. I then opened a cake, which was in one of the shopping bags. James came in just as I was clearing up and said "Do me some food Marie." I said I had enough to do, then he whacked me and punched me and said "I will have what you had." I didn't argue with him, as I knew he would beat me up and I was not in the mood, so I just did it. I told him what had happened and he went out and left me alone. Dad came in just as I cleared up again and asked what I was doing and where was Mam? He had been to the pub. I told him what had happened and he said "Well I can't go to the hospital now. Marie, has your Mam cooked my dinner? Did she do the shopping?" "Yes, I have just put it away and no there is not any dinner ready. The policeman took Mam to the hospital." "Which hospital?" I looked at him, "Why? Is there more than one hospital?" I said "I don't know which hospital no one told me. She hurt her leg really bad, there was lots of blood and it looked twisted to me with a bone sticking out. I heard the ambulance man say it was broken in 2 places; Dad can they mend broken bones? It was horrible, the fireman used a saw to remove the wooden planks." Dad said "The people at the hospital would fix it and why weren't you watching her, what have we told you about watching the young uns?" "Dad she was right with me and Robert went on the tall slide, so I was trying to watch both of them but June ran off to the roundabout whilst Robert was up the tall slide and she would have been alright but this boy spun it around very fast, I could not leave Robert the slide was as tall as a house." "Okay Marie it's not your fault; have you eaten? I'm starving, cook me some bacon and eggs and three slices of bread and butter." I did as I was asked. Then George came in and said "That smells nice, do me some Marie." Dad said "Do it yourself she is not a slave." *I was thinking that was exactly what I was, more like a servant, but what's new.* George nudged me when Dad went to sit down, he said "Do me some." I did it because I knew I would get a battering sooner or later. I burnt his toast so he yelled at me "Now do some more you stupid idiot!" Dad had eaten his dinner and he'd fallen asleep in the armchair so he did not hear how he spoke to me, not that he challenged George very often.

June was in hospital two weeks. She came out with her leg in a plaster cast from her thigh to her toes. Her leg had been broken in three places. She was fine and she laughed when we all drew funny pictures on it. She was soon feeling back to normal and doing her usual running around.

CHAPTER TWENTY TWO

SCARED OUT OF MY WITS

In early May 1965 I went on our usual Saturday morning trip to the park with Robert, June and Carol in the pram. Mam gave me a bottle of water and a packet of biscuits. Sometimes she would give us a bag of broken biscuits from a box she got really cheap. We all liked the custard creams best. This was usual for a Saturday with a sixpence for some sweets from a shop down the lane. The sweet shop had rows upon rows of jars of every kind of sweet you could imagine. I always bought a sixpenny mix of hard-boiled sweets. The man was very nice and said "Off to the park again young lady?" I would just nod at him. Our sixpence bought us about two ounces of sweets but the man always put a few extra in for good luck. I didn't understand what he meant but he often said that. I always asked for more fruit sweets otherwise he put mints in and we did not like those. Our sweets would last all day. We had a great day; it was sunny and dry on this occasion so we played, climbed trees and made some new friends. It's easy to make friends well not real friends, as we never saw them twice, when you're young you kind of just join in we just chatted and joined in and we often stayed until the sun went down. I felt kind of free when on the park.

This particular Saturday it was well into the afternoon and time to leave. There were several entrances and exits to the park and I chose one I had never used before to come off the park, a bit of a short cut. It came out facing the Red Lion where I went with me Dad. At the back of the pub there was a pig farm, which often had sheep and young lambs almost in the garden of the pub. Coming out this way saved time by not having to walk along the main road and we could run in and out the trees which we liked. There were lots of old dead tree stumps across the dirt pathway, which made it hard to push the pram, so sometimes I would leave it whilst we played hide and seek. Never in my wildest dreams did I think anything bad would happen.

I was walking along having had a really nice day with Robert now holding onto the pram and the other two girls in the pram. He always knew never to let go whilst we were walking. Robert and I were singing nursery rhymes and Carol was fast asleep. June with her bright pink rosy cheeks was slumped next to Carol's face; she too was drifting off to sleep, as they were exhausted after playing all day. Every time the pram went over a bump in the ground their heads rubbed against each other so I stopped in order to make them more comfortable. Whilst I was seeing to them I heard a rustling noise in the trees. Robert looked up at me and said "Marie I don't like going home this way." I looked around and guessed it must have been a rabbit or bird the bushes were quite dense either side of the path so there would have been all sorts of animals scurrying about. I said "It's alright it's just an animal in the woods." It was getting late and the tall overhanging trees made it look a little darker than it really was, I suddenly felt nervous myself trying not to show it to Robert. I shrugged it off and carried on walking and then all at once a man jumped out from the bush and grabbed my hand. He pulled so hard I had to let go of the pram sending the pram rocking from side to side on its springs. I thought it was going to tip over. I heard June moan and Robert looked really frightened I heard him cry Marie. The man said, "They will be alright." I said "No" but he pushed me to the ground behind a bush. I fell to my knees, and he knelt in front of me. I just thought of Robert hanging onto the pram, "Oh God keep them safe" I said out loud without realising it. The man laughed at me and said, "Yes God will look after them and you can look after me."

The man was about 40 with an unshaven face. He was wearing grey scruffy trousers and a dingy coloured shirt. His hair was scruffy looking as it hung down just below his ears. I noticed he had little potholes all over his face and he stank of booze. As he stood there he started to undo his trousers and he said, "Have you seen one of these before?" It stood proud in his trousers. As I pulled away the fear engulfed me. I could not speak. He said, "Just wank me off and I will give you half a crown which is a lot of money, then you can go back to them kids and get off home." I had no idea what the word wank meant, so I looked away I had to keep my wits about me or goodness know what would happen I said this in my head, then he grabbed my hand and said "If you don't help me out I will do it to you properly and it will hurt you and when I've finished with you I'll do it to those bloody kids do you understand me?" My fear grew into horror and I knew I had to get away from him. He was a bad man and I thought he might kill us all and bury us in the dense undergrowth. All I could smell was booze and fags as he pulled my hand towards his thing. He was just out of reach and he said, "Move closer I am not going to hurt you." His trousers fell down around his knees whilst he was trying to pull me closer; I kind of shuffled but lifted my feet and stood up. My heart was pounding and something inside told me to run. I got up in a jerking motion as if to move closer and pushed him over, I ran towards the path, shouting, "Help me, help me" as I ran. I heard him trying to get up and he shouted, "I'll get you, I know where you live you little bastard." In my panic I grabbed Robert, put him on the pram on top of June and ran towards the exit of the park. Luckily it was not too far but it was very bumpy with all the tree roots underground across the pathway. I stumbled a couple of times but managed to steady the pram and myself. The man never came after me and once I was on the main road, my heart slowed down and I began to cry. Robert asked, "Was he a bad man Marie?" I did not answer him; *my thoughts were racing out of control. What if he killed me, what if I hadn't run away, what if he hurt the young uns, why did he choose me, why do I get picked on at school, why, why, why, what if, what if? By now I was sobbing.*

Robert interrupted my sobbing and said "Marie does the bad man know where we live, will he come and get you, Marie he said he will find you shall I tell Mam?"

I said "No and please don't tell Mam, or we will not be able to go out again, it's okay Robert we are safe and yes he was a bad man and he was a drunk."

Mam was at home when we arrived but I went straight to my room and lay down on my bed and sobbed some more. Mam never found out and I held another secret. I did see the man once or twice in the area he lived a few streets away I think? But I never had the courage to tell Mam, and besides, no one would have believed me, in those days they didn't.

I did not go to that park for several months. I only started to go on the park again because some other kids asked me to go with them. I hesitated for a long time before saying yes. I thought that if we all stayed together I would be safe even though I was very nervous. My need to start playing with other kids was greater and this helped me to push my previous encounter with the bad man to the back of my mind.

CHAPTER TWENTY THREE

CHAPEL ST LEONARD'S

During the following year things changed somewhat. We went on a holiday to Chapel St-Leonard's and we all stayed in a caravan. It was nice inside with sofas, which could turn into beds. The windows all had green flowery curtains, which matched the sofas, and they were on opposite sides of the van with a small table separating them. There was a separate bedroom with a bed and wardrobes. There was a small bedroom, which housed bunk beds, with only just enough room to get out of bed. A tiny kitchen with an oven, hob and fridge were in the main walkway from the door and there was a tiny little gas fire in the lounge area. It reminded me of an oversized dolls house. I thought it was really nice.

Mam had warned us all to keep the van tidy, and the first sign of arguing and we were home on the next bus, and Mam meant every word.

We went as a family, which was also nice, Mam, Dad, James, Robert, June, Carol and myself. Dad's benevolent fund from the pit paid for this holiday too. I heard it said it was for families who were not very well off, or for families who needed a holiday because they had problems. We seemed to fit in both categories on this occasion. It was nice when we were all together, relaxed and having a good time. The beach was fun we built sand castles, which were very good with moats running around the perimeter we tried very hard to keep them full, but the water just got absorbed in the sand. It was hard for the young ones to understand where the water was going. Then James came up with the idea of lining the moat with plastic bags, so the water stayed put for a while and we had flags sticking out of each turret, and beautiful gateways lined with shells and stones. We spent all day building sand castles linking them altogether.

There was an amusement arcade with slot machines for rainy days. We did not have much to spend so we looked in all the money trays where the winning cash came out of the machine if you won. We would follow someone who was winning and sometimes they'd give us a penny to go away. We often found the odd penny left in the tray where people had not collected all their winnings, which meant we could have another try in the hope we would win. In the evening we all went to the on site club where there were lots of activities for everyone. I remember we had a fancy dress evening for the kids. Robert entered as a coal miner and I entered as a salad girl. My dress was made out of green crepe paper with tomatoes, cucumber, onions and radishes, sewn all over it. Everything was made from crepe paper except the giant bow around my waist, which tied at the back. This was a beautiful yellow satin ribbon and I wore a bow in my hair to match. Mam made it all, she was so creative. My brother Robert won first prize and I came second. My prize was a handbag which I carried everywhere, I loved it. Robert's prize was a voucher, which he could spend in the shop on the caravan site, and we both had our photos taken for the local newspaper. We were so special no one knew the torment we suffered at home and for those few days life was good.

There were no beatings for James and Dad could hardly touch me in a caravan. Dad still went to the pub at lunchtime but he left me alone. Mam had a good time too, going off to bingo whenever she could, leaving me with Robert who was then seven, June who was four and Carol who was just under three. As children we all enjoyed the beach. I spent most of the holiday watching the young ones, but I did not mind, in fact I enjoyed it. The tide was out so far I could hardly see the sea and the beach went on for miles in both directions, close by to where we were there were 6 donkeys which plodded up and down the beach with kids on them the donkeys all had different names the man guided them with a stick but I never saw him strike them he touched them on the bum if they refused to budge.

Mam had never left me on the beach for more than half an hour before. It was a Thursday and I remember James had made friends with another boy who was also on holiday staying on the same caravan site. He used to ask if he could stay and play with his new friend and later he went to the zoo with his friend and his parents.

We found a nice place on the beach and Dad set up a windbreaker, then Dad left us at 12 o'clock to go to the pub and shortly after that Mam said "I'm going to bingo now, I will be gone for about an hour." That was at 1.30 and she went on to say "Now you look after them, don't take your eyes off them, you're growing up and you need to take some responsibility now be a good girl" and off she went not telling me where, other than she was going to bingo.

I was left, with a bottle of water, a cheese sandwich each, a packet of biscuits and a few sweets. We all held hands running in and out of the water, although Carol was not yet 3 years old. Carol was sturdy on her feet but she kept falling down which made her laugh and cry at the same time, she also cried if I let go of her hand. She was really scared of the sea but felt safe holding onto me but then I slipped and fell and they all jumped on top of me, I had sand in my swimming costume and we all giggled, splashed and collected water in our buckets for the sand castles, the four of us played happily. We had our picnic and I was watching the others playing nicely. Mam had brought me a comic called Judy which I read whilst they were piling up mounds of sand until a hill formed. The two girls buried Robert's legs so just his upper body was visible. It looked so funny we were all laughing and people around us were laughing too.

There was a man nearby on the beach talking loudly to a crowd of people. As I looked over I could see the crowd beginning to swell from all sides. Eventually the preacher man was completely surrounded. I was drawn to his voice and I stood up to see what was happening. As I moved closer I found myself hypnotised by this man's voice. I sat on some steps so I could still see the young uns playing whilst listening to the man. I soon lost myself in the words of the evangelist saying that God was the only way, Jesus loved us all, no matter what sin we had done, Jesus forgives all. He died to save each and every one of us and is calling each one of us now to

97

follow Him. I liked what I heard and I wanted to hear more. I listened for about half an hour while he told the story about Jesus on the mountain when he shared the loaves of bread and fish. *I sat and imagined this was Jesus in front of me giving out the fish and loaves of bread to hungry people. I wanted him to say I will be your friend, but this was an ordinary man not Jesus. How does he know that Jesus knows me, or wants to be my friend and how does Jesus know I am a sinner. Does he know about my Dad and if he knows everything like this man said, why can't he stop the horrible things happening? I wanted to shout out to the man "Help me" but I knew my life would not be worth living if my Dad found out that I'd let the secret out.* My mind was going into overdrive thinking about this Jesus, the things I was hearing, and the things I had been taught in school and Sunday school.

I was in a bit of a daze because of the bright sunshine and the crowd, which had gathered. I suddenly looked up and I could no longer see the man or my brother and sisters. I was completely surrounded by what seemed like hundreds of people. I looked around and could not see the children anymore. I wanted so much to stay but knew I had to get back to the spot where I had left them. I suddenly started to panic and with good reason, I got back to where I'd left the children and noticed there were only two of them. Panic and fear went through me as I shouted, "Where is Carol?" Robert said "She went down to get some water for the moat, look Marie the sand keeps drinking it; do you like the castle Marie?" Although I could hear Robert I was not listening to him as my eyes went straight to the edge of the sea looking for Carol.

I remember hearing the crowd sing *"This little light of mine, I'm gonna let it shine."* I could just hear the din of the singers. In my sheer panic-stricken brain, I ignored Robert's words and grabbed both his and June's hands and shouted at them, "Look for Carol, Robert can you see her?" She was nowhere to be seen. The beach was crowded and it seemed to be getting bigger with each step we took. I looked up and down the shoreline. There were some children playing in the waves and some sitting at the waters edge on the beach, but none of them were as small as Carol, "Robert how long has she been gone was it soon after I moved or after?" Being children they had no concept of time. I would never know how long she had been gone.

The sun was still shining and my eyes hurt with staring out to sea. I began to worry, my heart was thumping, and then I saw a lifeguard and said, "I have lost my sister please help." I told the lifeguard that Carol went down to the water's edge to collect some water for our sand castles and that I could not find her now. His first words were "Where are your parents?" I told him that Dad was in the pub and Mam was at bingo but that I didn't know where. "I can't find Carol, I know where the caravan is. It's across the main road and around the corner. Please help me find her; she is only two and a half. Where can she be? I can't see her anywhere."

The lifeguard must have seen I was very scared. He started talking into his radio and within a few minutes there were about six policemen with binoculars, looking out to sea. I was petrified. I stood there saying "Please God if you are there, keep her safe."

One police officer asked me if I knew where we were staying. I said over the road in a caravan. I was asked to go back to the caravan to see if she had made it back. "How would she know at that age to go back to the van she won't be there." "Now do as we say you would be surprised the sense children have." I held onto Robert and June's hands and rushed them to the caravan site. A policeman came with us but when we arrived the caravan was empty so I scratched in the dirt on the door.

Mam, contact the police Carol has gone missing!

What could I do, we were all upset. Robert and June were crying and asking me where Carol had gone. Robert asked if Carol had drowned, I said, "I don't know." I was trying to quieten them down when a woman from the caravan next to ours came out. I told her what had happened and she very kindly offered to take Robert and June into her caravan. I had to agree, although I did not really know her but because the policeman was there I figured it would be all right. It was for the best as June had to be carried everywhere by this time as she was getting tired. I said "Robert be good for the lady I have to look for Carol. Mam will be back soon, thank you Mrs." As I walked off I could hear June crying. I ran as fast as I could across the road to the beach. I found it hard to run on the sand but rushed trying to keep up with the policeman, my steps flicking sand onto peoples towels as I passed them still sunbathing. By the time I got to the water's edge there was a full-scale search in progress with policemen and women and volunteers all looking out to sea and some through their binoculars. My heart was thumping so hard I thought it was going to split my chest wide open but I held back my tears and went to the man I had already spoken to.

A policewoman came to me and said "Don't worry we will find her." She put her arm on my shoulder and went on to ask me lots of questions about Carol. I told her what she was wearing: a full swimsuit in yellow with little pink flowers on it and that it was too big for her because it was June's. She has short blonde hair. I said, "I am sure she would not go into the sea because she is scared of it." I began to cry and mumble at the same time "What if someone has taken her, please find my Mam." "We have policemen trying to find your Mam as we speak don't worry." *I thought how can I not worry it's my fault she has gone, what trouble was I in. What if she is dead, what if she has been taken, what if she went up the beach towards the road and has been run over by a bus and was lying in hospital all alone, My thoughts were ongoing thinking the worst, with what ifs.*

The policewoman interrupted my thoughts and asked my name and then said "Marie you must try to be calm. I know you are scared but we need your help, I need a few answers now be sensible I am sure your Mam would not have left you if she did not think you were sensible and capable. Does your Mam play bingo in the arcades or in a bingo hall?" I said she played in the arcades where she wins prizes because she saves them for Christmas presents. She got on the radio and told the others. "Now do you know where your Dad is drinking?" I nodded no. "Did he drive to the pub?" Again I nodded no. She radioed again "Dad must be local to the caravan site, try The Bull then try The Crown." She said, "Now can you tell me where you were before Carol went missing," I said "Yes, I was listening to the preacher man." She said "No I mean the children." I knew the exact spot as there were two enormous sand castles and our towel was still on the sand with the bottle of half drank water. I began to cry with a shaking voice I asked if Carol was in the sea. She said "Well we do not know yet but I doubt it as you said she does not really like the sea, do you think she would paddle alone?" I nodded no. "Now Marie I want you to know that whatever happens here today it's not your fault." I replied it was. "I was not watching them, and I was listening to the preacher man. I could see them at first but then lots of people blocked my view, Mam will go mad at me it will be my fault you do not know me Mam." She smiled and said, "I will have a word, now be a good girl and show me where you were and where the children were playing." We walked up the beach until we arrived at the spot. The towel was almost buried with sand because people had trampled on it, but I knew it was ours. The buckets, spades, flags, shells and the wind breaker were all still there as if nothing was wrong and we would all return to play with them after the fuss was over.

It was now well into the afternoon and the sun was going behind some clouds, though it was still nice and warm. I began to shiver or tremble; I could not be sure which. The policewoman told me to pick up all our things and we will go to the caravan. She helped me pick up our stuff and we walked across the road, around the corner and onto the caravan site. We went by the site supermarket, then by a park area where we stopped to look, just in case Carol had found her way there. There were lots of children playing but no sign of Carol.

As we arrived at our caravan we met two more policemen, who had been walking around the site. One of them said, "We've found the mother, she is on her way with PC Smedley." I immediately spotted Mam rushing across the caravan site, she was yelling "Marie wait till I get hold of you." She was like a mad woman possessed. As she approached, she said "What were you doing taking your eyes off them? I warned you." Then she looked at the van. "You've scratched the van, fancy writing on the van you stupid girl I can't leave you for ten minutes, and we will have to pay for that." Then she asked where the others were, but before I could tell her they came down the steps of the other van, running towards me. Mam just looked and said "Oh no, now the whole site knows our business, your Dad will go mad. Oh Marie what have you done?"

I could tell Mam was not just angry; she had tears in her eyes with worry. She bellowed "What were you doing? I told you to look after them, I left you for just ten minutes, now where did you go, you left them didn't you?" Robert said "She only left us for a little while and we could see her all the time." She came towards me pointing into my face and I burst into tears. Mam said "Yes you will cry my girl" and she clouted me across the head so hard it threw my head to the side, banging it on the caravan.

The policewoman tried to calm Mam down and said "Look this is not helping at all. Your concern should be for Carol after all Marie is only eleven herself." Mam replied, "What are you saying? That I've neglected my children?" The policewoman ignored her and then asked the woman in the next van if I could go around there for a while. She agreed and I went off sobbing. But Mam was shouting horrible things after me. The policewoman said that her priority was to find the child and that all this blaming and anger was not helping the situation, it did not matter who was to blame. After a while Mam calmed down and the policewoman explained what she thought had happened and that there were loads of police officers out looking for Carol, combing the beach and the town and that they were also looking for Dad. Mam said, "He will go mad as he's been to the pub. Oh God when he's had a drink, he goes mad." She was asked which pub he was in. "The Bull," Mam replied.

I sat on the steps of the van with a drink of orange and could hear the conversation. Here's the Dad, Serge, one of them said. He had had a few beers but he still looked in control. He looked at Mam with daggers in his eyes, and then all at once the policewoman said, "We've found the little girl, we think she's on her way, she said her name was Carol, so let's be hopeful." About ten minutes later, a policeman rode up on a black bicycle with Carol sitting in front of him. Carol was smiling and holding a biscuit. The policeman said she was found about a mile up the beach. She had crossed the road and was going onto the Chapel caravan site when a woman found her. She took her back to her caravan, gave her a drink and a biscuit then she phoned us. He said that she was a friendly and very chatty little girl but he went on to tell us how lucky we were and how something really bad could have happened. He ended his lecture by saying that we should all have learnt a lesson from this ordeal.

Mam said thank goodness and Dad went over and took her off the bike and hugged her, then passed her to Mam who asked her if she was okay. She smiled and said in her language "Been on a bike, want to go to Marie." Mam half smiled back, hugged her and said "Go to your sister." Carol had no idea she had been lost or how worried we all were. Mam put her down and she ran over to me, I hugged her and said I was sorry then June came and sat on my other knee we all hugged each other.

The policemen all went away, the crisis was over, or at least it was for them. We all returned to the caravan and Dad went crazy at Mam. "What were you doing woman, leaving them on the beach for hours with Marie? For God's sake what were you thinking of?" She shouted back "Well you can talk you haven't been out of the pub since we got here." Mam blamed me and struck out but missed, and said to Dad "Your precious little girl was listening to a preacher man." Dad said "No! This is you we are talking about. She is only eleven." Mam shouted back "Yes and it would do for you to remember she's only eleven too." "And what do you mean by that?" "You know what I mean," Mam mumbled, "I knew it couldn't be her fault, Daddy's little girl, she can never do anything wrong in your eyes."

Although I was listening I dared not speak and anyway I was sobbing too hard to even talk. This was my entire fault, I was causing a massive row and the whole of the caravan park must have heard. I left the room and threw myself on the bed. Robert and June soon followed me. I was sobbing and June put her arms around me and said "Marie I love you don't cry." Then Robert hugged me and said "Sorry Marie." I looked at him blurry eyed and said you're not to blame Robert, I should not have left you, and it was all entirely my fault. They both snuggled close and we lay there until Mam and Dad stopped shouting. The holiday was ruined and it was my doing. I just wanted to go home and two days later we did.

Chapter Twenty -Four

The Enormous Turkey

Mam was very popular with the neighbours and had lots of friends. She knitted and made all our clothes and also knitted hours upon hours for anyone who asked her, especially in the run up to Christmas because it meant she could earn a few bob for extras like another night at bingo with her friends in the hope that she could win more gifts for us.

With 7 children, a demanding husband and a part time job her pleasures in life were few. She did not laugh very often but I recall one Christmas Day when the dining room was laid out for dinner. Mam and Dad had really gone to town this particular year; money must have been plentiful. Dad, along with my brother George built a bar in the corner of the room, which they stocked with all different types of spirits, wines and beers. They even put Christmas fairy lights all around the shelf; they truly looked the business.

Everyone arrived at more or less the same time but there seemed to be more people than usual. I remember the two aunties with their husbands, Grandma and a friend of Dad's who lived on his own. He was a very funny man and he was always smiling. He said "I feel honoured to be here in this wonderful home." He enjoyed his drink just like dad; he was probably one of Dad's drinking crony's from the pub. With all of us the house was bursting at the seams. The drink began to flow and everyone was getting merrier the more they drank. The tables were laid ready for dinner and no one was ever with an empty glass.

What Dad did not know was that Mam and Aunt Bess were pouring their drinks into the large potted plant, which stood nearby. They gave each other a crafty smile as they did it. They talked about Christmas's gone by and Mam said "He's had a joint of ham soaking in a bucket for a week. He cooked it all night on the gas stove in the same bucket. The heat and length of time it was on the cooker must have burnt through the bottom of the bucket, this is all whilst we were asleep mind. He got up this morning to find the ham stuck welded to the top of the cooker. He managed to rescue the top half but it's a wonder we are here to tell the tale, the stupid sod. He must have been drunk to even think it would be alright on the cooker all night." Aunt Bess laughed and asked, "Will it be OK? I can't smell burning; usually you can smell it for days." Mam shrugged her shoulders and said "Shush he'll hear us, you know how bad tempered he can be if he thinks we are talking about him." Dad shouted, "Are you two empty again? You must be pissed up by now. You're both giggling. It's nice to see you both happy." They both looked at my other Aunt and they all burst out laughing together.

You see Dad would never take no for an answer; he got drunk so everyone else had too. The plant did at any rate.

Dad asked me to turn on the radio so we could listen to the Christmas carols. He said, "Right has everyone got a full glass?" Those who did not have a drink hastily filled their glasses up. The candles were lit in the table centrepiece, which was beautifully dressed with holly and poinsettia flowers, one of Mam's favourites. The vegetables were in dishes on the table and the huge turkey was about to make its debut.

The smells coming from the kitchen were amazing we were all very hungry it's funny how smells attack the taste buds.

The turkey was on a massive ceramic platter it was sitting with pride golden brown with rashers of streaky bacon carefully placed over the breast it was stuffed with his home made chestnut and Bramley apple stuffing plugged with a whole cooking onion. Dad said it kept the moisture in the bird. It was surrounded with all sorts of other food: mini sausages again with bacon wrapped around them. Dad was so proud of his cooking it smelt delicious. It was the biggest turkey we had ever seen and it took all night to cook. Dad walked in with the platter held tight in both hands he said this is the biggest and best turkey we have ever had. Then just as he was walking through the doorway with one foot on the ground the other foot stood directly on to one of the children's toys. His knee bent and he fell awkwardly sending the turkey flying off the platter up into the air. It was so funny it was just like something out of a comedy strip. We must have all looked a picture, some of us laughed; some of us looked in horror as the turkey took flight and fell to the lino clad floor splattering the walls and anyone sitting nearby with stuffing, sausages, roast potatoes and turkey juices.

Dad's face was mixed with anger, horror and pain because he was well oiled from the Whiskey he'd been drinking all morning. He managed a half smile but what else could he do with a house full of people. The room fell silent apart from the radio playing the carol Joy to the World. No one moved a muscle, and then Dad burst out laughing and in turn everyone else followed. Everyone's face was gradually changing from total shock to cackles of laughter. Dad and Mam picked up the turkey, stuffing, sausages and roast potatoes, dusted them all off and represented them on the same unbroken platter which was a miracle and no one suffered the consequences. Except the bird that fell apart on the floor but Dad put it back together the best he could and we all ate until we couldn't eat anymore. Anyone walking in at that moment would not have known the bird had just taken flight.

As Dad began to carve the turkey breast he said "Right who left the toy in the doorway or was it planted there deliberately by you little buggers? Who had the toy for Christmas?" No one answered because no one dared to answer. Was he joking? We could never tell, as he was always so volatile and unpredictable when drunk. Then all at once June let out a squeal of laughter and said "Me, it was me. I was playing and left it on the floor." Everyone laughed hysterically including Dad.

Then all at once Aunt Bess said "Have we got a ham for tea like always?" Mam nudged her under the table. Dad looked at Mam and said "Alright so I burnt the bloody ham there is a hole in my bucket and yes, it's ok and we will be eating it for tea." He smirked at Mam and the merriment went on with us all singing *There's a hole in my bucket dear Liza, dear Liza.*

My other Auntie said "Well this is one lovely dinner, do we all agree?" We all did agree and clapped our hands together thanking Dad for all his hard work.

I made a Christmas cake for a competition at school. It took weeks and weeks to make and instead of a Christmas scene made from icing I made it into a birthday cake for Mam. I decorated it with poinsettia flowers in one corner and I iced Happy Birthday Mam in dark pink icing across the middle. My cake did not win the competition because it was not officially a Christmas cake but the judges who were my school teachers said it was really lovely. Mam's birthday was on Christmas Eve and she shed some tears when she saw it as I had forfeited my position in the competition. Dad said "We should save it to show everyone on Christmas Day." Mam was so proud of me and I only wanted to please her because I loved her.

CHAPTER TWENTY FIVE

REX

We now had an Alsatian dog named Rex; he had longish brown hair and stood very tall with a huge jaw. He was very friendly and playful; we had him from a puppy. He grew to love us and we loved him back. Rex was the best thing to happen to us this year and as he grew into an adult dog Dad made a sledge and harness so he could pull the little ones up and down the street in the snow. I watched them all having lots of fun and although we all played with him he actually belonged to George. George and Dad treated Rex like a gun dog. They took him shooting, bringing home wood pigeons and the odd wild rabbit. Dad plucked or skinned them, cooking them very slowly in the oven and making very big pies with their kill. He used some of his homegrown vegetables and it was a good meal. Some of the family moaned and refused to eat them, saying it tasted off. Dad cursed and said game was strong in flavour and how could it be off when they were freshly killed. I liked pigeon pie, and I enjoyed eating rabbit, usually in the form of stew. In fact I liked Dad's cooking and later went on to be a good cook myself with a taste for game. Anyway it beat the bad times when all we got to eat was a plate of dark green cabbage, nothing else, just cabbage. I loved food but not cabbage. I was forced to sit and eat it gagging at the thought of it. Dad made me sit there until it was all gone and then he forced the last bit into my mouth even hours later when it was stone cold. "You will not move until that plate is clean, none of you." I was crying at the table but eventually we had no choice and I would eat it but out of sheer frustration. I would then make myself sick in the toilet which became a habit since making myself sick started to make me feel better.

I suppose I took after Dad where food was concerned, as he loved meat and so did I. Mam was not a good cook at all. Her dinners consisted mainly of tinned or processed foods. I learned to cook while very young, which did not do me any harm. We were all healthy and well covered and did not often go too hungry.

I never knew why but Rex was put down. I heard he bit a child, which did not make sense as we played with him all the time. We would sit Carol and June on his back just like you would sit on a pony. We lay on him, dressed him in our clothes, pulled him about, you name it we did it to him. How could he have bitten another child? Anyway he was gone like everything else, taken from us.

There was not much peace at home. Dad got drunk most nights and Mam had mood swings, she never seemed to be at home. George fell out with Dad on a daily basis, which often ended up in punch ups on the lawn, brawling like two complete strangers. No words were spoken, just fists flying. Sometimes they had an audience with the neighbours looking on. Dad enjoyed the attention, and he could look after himself and invariably won giving George a bloody nose. George said he felt guilty for hitting his own Dad. Dad shouted to the onlookers "You can go in now it's over." Eventually George left home.

John did not come home at all that year not even to visit, and I missed having him to talk to. I really missed him, he was my friend as well as my brother and I could talk to him. Mam was not easy to talk to these days, as she was too ill. All I got were my orders as she said, "Marie do this, Marie do that." In fact it felt to me as though everyone said Marie do this or Marie do that. I was a servant to my family captured in a horror story, never allowed to express how I felt. Although James and I used to be good friends, we seemed to squabble and fight on a daily basis. In fact all day would be nearer to the truth, he would hit me more, and the more he hit me the harder the punches got.

James would force me to fetch and carry for him until I feared being alone with him. He would constantly make me jump by hiding then shouting as I walked by grabbing me in the process. I actually feared him.

One time James put a pillow over my face, because I refused to move off the chair that he wanted to sit on. He held it so tight I feared I was going to die of suffocation. Even today I always sleep with my bed covers below my shoulders, as I get panicky when my head is covered.

If Dad heard us James would get a beating. Dad always trapped him in the corner like an animal then out came the poky stick. James could not get away from Dad, who just struck him across his back, legs, arms and bottom. Dad never knew when to stop and it just went around full circle. James hit me then he got beat up by way of a punishment by Dad who enjoyed being the circus master watching as James squirmed in the corner.

I was just 12 and our family felt like it was falling apart. Dad would call me to his bedroom on a regular basis. He would take hold of my hand and when he fell to sleep I left the room. I often lay awake at night as I worried about my schoolwork, worried about my life. Dad said I was his comfort and his special, favourite little girl. When I asked him why I didn't have a best friend he just said I am your best friend and you have the children, that's all you need, you have us.

Mam got really sick and had to go back into hospital. She had to have chemotherapy every week for several weeks but the children didn't understand or know what it was until years later.

I recall one particular day when I went home from school because I felt unwell myself. My illness continued for a number of days and gradually worsened with severe stomach pains. After the third day Mam insisted on calling for the doctor and both Mam and Dad were in when the doctor examined me. He pushed and prodded my tummy until I squealed. He said, "Hospital for you my dear, I suspect you have appendicitis." I overheard him saying to Mam that I needed an operation today as my appendix was inflamed and that I could get peritonitis if it was left any longer. He told Mam that there was not enough time to wait for an ambulance so he took me in his car. Mam rushed around getting a nightgown and toothbrush together and before we knew it I was sat in the doctor's car on my way to hospital.

I had two weeks in hospital after my appendix had been removed which was not too bad. I was laid up in bed for a few days, with about eight stitches on my right side. The nurses were very kind and as soon as I could I was out of bed helping them in whichever way I was able. They thought it was unusual how a young girl could make tea and generally be such a good help. I remember them saying I was a special little girl. Whilst I liked being called special it worried me, as I was always Dad's special little girl. I wondered what was expected of me so I stopped helping so much. Anyway I did not really see their point in praising me like they did, as this is what I did all the time at home and I never remember being thanked by members of my family. It was not too difficult, no task was too great, and I was told I should be resting but I always wanted to please others.

I was off school a total of six weeks during which Mam taught me to iron the more difficult items of clothing like shirts and trousers and showed me numerous other tasks around the home. She also taught me how to knit using up all the odd balls of wool and I eventually made a blanket out of the squares of different colours. It looked nice and Carol liked it so much she had it on her bed. I also learned how to use the sewing machine.

Six weeks of learning different things made the time go by very quickly. I really enjoyed our time together and I was not afraid of hard work, as I had been used to it from a very early age. I wanted to tell her so much about what Dad was doing, but she would always interrupt my thoughts. Then one day she said "You will be in charge of the household chores one day." I laughed and said "I am now what do you mean?" She looked a little sad and said "If I show you something I do not want you to be upset and there is no need to tell anyone else."

Another secret I thought. "I feel it's time you knew why my asking for your help has increased." She said "Come with me upstairs." When we got to her bedroom she lifted her dress up. I said "Mam what yer doing?" Mam had a big tummy and large hanging breasts due to all the children she bore. She had no bra on to hold them in place and I felt a little embarrassed, so I tried not to look in too much detail. She always wore very big knickers, which she slid down to reveal her pubic bone not that it was visible, as her skin was unrecognisable as a part of her body. As I looked I turned away, as I felt her pain with the scars that were in front of me.

The tears ran down my cheeks as I asked, "Mam what was it all for, why are you being sliced up like a piece of meat?" Mam said, "I have been ill for a long time as you know Marie ever since Carol was born. In fact it was even before that really. I've had operation after operation to try to make me better." "And have they made you better Mam?" Mam replied in a quiet tone "I hope so, I do hope so." Then in an even quieter voice, which I could only just hear, "For the sake of you children I do hope so." "What Mam, what did you say?" She answered "Nothing Marie." Her voice was quivering as if she wanted to cry. I had heard her crying before, usually when Dad was shouting or forcing her to do things in the bedroom late at night. She then pulled her knickers up, dropped her dress and gave me a tight hug. "Marie everything will be alright, come on let's clean up downstairs before yer Dad gets home, you know what he is like."

Chapter Twenty Six

FEAR

I overheard Mam and Dad having sex on several occasions. There is nothing wrong with that after all they were married. It was just that we could hear everything. I suppose it was inevitable someone would overhear things in a three-bedroom house, but this time was different. Mam was crying fairly loudly and I heard her saying "No, no I can't, I'm not well, you know I am not well and besides Marie is still awake." Why would she say that when James was also in bed and probably awake too? In fact all us kids were in bed. Maybe she said it because my bed was closest to the wall although there was a stairwell in between. Dad said, "So what she knows what it's about." Mam cried a little louder and she said "But you're hurting me please stop." I could tell Dad was forcing her, then there was a loud slap and I heard Mam crying loudly. It seemed to go on for ages. I put the pillow over my ears and lay in my bed trying not to listen. I know the girls and Robert were asleep but was James? I wanted so much for him to be near me, just to say it's alright, it's what grown ups do, but he was in another room. I prayed to God to make Dad stop, but God was just not listening, he never heard my prayers. What was the point? He just could not hear me, as my prayers were just in my head. I always prayed in vain. I wanted so much to shout "Leave her alone, just leave Mam alone," but I knew of the consequences. So Dad carried on and I carried on in silent prayer until I fell asleep.

I knew Mam was ill because she was in and out of the hospital all the time but I didn't appreciate just how serious it was. I cried silently for fear of waking the others. That night my sleep was very restless along with many others I encountered.

The next day Mam was out for the whole day at the hospital having treatment, something called chemotherapy and Dad said I had to stay home from school to help him. After everyone had left for either work or school he called me to his room and said, "Come and help me Marie I need you to help me." I looked at him lying there on the bed. He was wearing a dressing gown, which was not fastened, with just his underpants underneath. My heart thumped with fear as I entered the room. He said "Close the door and lock it," in a stern voice nothing gentle like at other times, "You know what will happen if you don't, and Mam does not need to be told. She is very ill you know and if you tell her it will make her worse." I did as I was asked and laid at his side, the fear engulfing me. I just did not want to touch it again, but today was to be different. He began to undress me, which he had never done before. It was usually me who had to touch him. I asked him to stop, for what good it did as it fell on deaf ears. Then he pushed my hand into a pot of Vaseline and again as usual wrapped my hand around his penis, with his hand firmly gripped on mine. I felt it growing in my small hand then he dipped his hand into the jar and began massaging my genitals. His other hand was firmly over my mouth so no one could hear my screams. He pushed my legs wide apart abruptly, hurting my thighs. I tried to push his hand away, but he forced my arm away and held it so I could not move until it hurt me to struggle. He warned me yet again, "You will all end up in care, if anyone finds out about you and me." Then he rolled over on top of me and began working his way inside of me. I said, "You're hurting me." He said, "That's what all you women say" *but "I am not a woman, I'm a child" I mumbled behind his hand.* He pressed his hand even harder over my mouth and I could hardly breathe. I was crying. The pillow under my head was wet with my tears. I could not move and the smell of cigarettes and stale booze on his stinking breath nauseated me. I felt I was going to be sick. He began moving up and down very slowly, telling me to relax, it does not hurt if you relax, and more Vaseline was added. He said, "This will help, it makes it sloppy see, then it will not hurt you so much." But it did hurt. He wriggled and bounced up and down for what seemed a lifetime, ripping and squirming inside my privates. He never looked at me, not once did he make eye contact with me. I think I could have been anyone.

I closed my eyes and totally blanked off into a coma like state. I am not sure if I passed out, as my memory is elusive. He finished with a moan and collapsed at the side. Then he tapped my leg and said, "You can go now and don't forget, you don't tell a soul and yer Mam does not need to know, she is too ill. It will only make her worse." He always said this, every time we were alone, even just in the kitchen or on the street. He would warn me to keep quiet; as it was my fault all this was happening.

After he told me to leave the room I went straight into the bathroom, locked the door and ran the bath as full as I dared. It was boiling hot, but I did not care, I climbed into the bath almost scalding myself. I felt no pain from the hot water; my legs were scarlet as I scrubbed at my body with the nailbrush and green carbolic soap. The whole of my body tingled with pain. The water became pink. I did not know at first where the blood had come from. I looked at myself and realised I was bleeding from inside my private parts. I cried silently as I feared he would come in to fetch me again worried he would break the door down to get me, and not knowing what was happening to me, I lay there for what seemed hours. The pink water eventually became cold. I was shivering, scared of what was happening to me and knew my silence had to be kept. I got out the bath, wrapped a towel around myself and without drying myself properly I put on my dressing gown. I went to my bed where I just lay, staring at the top bunk, not thinking, not hearing, not seeing, just staring. I believe this was when the secret was first buried, put in the depths of my mind where no one could find it, not even me.

CHAPTER TWENTY SEVEN

NIGHTMARES

The same event became a ritual whenever Mam was out for the day at the hospital having her treatment. If I was not just touching him, he was touching me. He always said there was no point in him sitting around the hospital all day, so he didn't go with Mam even though he knew she was really ill.

I knew what to expect. He would write a note for me to take to school either for the morning or afternoon, briefly saying Mam was very ill and he needed me home. He got away with it time and time again. My pain got less and less and I only bled occasionally and my thoughts were of nothing. I managed somehow to block out what was happening. No one could help me, not even God, who I believed in, who I prayed to every night. I just accepted what was happening because I did not know how to stop it. Dad told me all the young uns, myself included, would all have to go into a home and that if Mam knew, it would send her into hospital again and that it would kill her if she knew. He said Mam was too ill to cope with my lies and that I should never speak of it ever. He said that no one would believe me if I told them and that he would deny it and that he would be believed because he was an adult and I would be sent into a home for naughty children who told horrible lies about their family. So it happened again and again. I don't know how but I managed to cope and somehow I got on with my life. My school was also blocked out from my memory as I remember very little from those years. I do not remember many of the other school children's names. I can remember I went to a girl's house down the road, you could call us friends but the memories are few. It's funny how the horrors of life remain a memory and yet school was just not there for me. It's almost like I never went to junior school at all.

I began having the same recurring nightmares night after night. I was all on my own trapped in a room, with the walls closing in a few inches at a time, until the two walls were touching either side of my body. Then the ceiling started to move slowly downwards. I was being crushed, squashed to death, unable to move as fear engulfed my whole body. Then I would wake up suffocating, gasping for air, panicking and crying, but my body was stiff with fear. I would be freezing cold but wet with sweat and could not get the walls to part. I needed to get out but couldn't, so I would scream for help. No one could hear me as I screamed and I tried to kick at the wall but to no avail, my screams could not be heard through the thick walls. I sobbed in fear. Mam would hear me on occasions and sometimes come in to my room and say, "It's just a dream Marie, calm down". I was terrified, shaking and crying. Mam suggested to Dad that I should sleep with them for a while and of course he agreed, but I was so scared Dad would touch me while Mam was in the same bed, whilst she was sleeping. I feared that even more, more than the nightmare itself so I said no I was okay. *I was lying, I was not okay, and I needed someone to hold me, someone to care, to know what was happening to me, I needed my fear to stop both in my dreams and in reality.*

I began to feel ill with constant soreness in my private area but like most things I kept this to myself. The fear of what would happen every time Mam left the house engulfed me. Then I got tonsillitis time after time; it was recurring week after week. Mam insisted to Dad I should see a doctor but Dad argued saying I was all right, and no doctor was needed. "Get her some mixture he would say". After having the same sore throat for a few weeks Mam started to get very worried and so she went behind Dad's back and asked the doctor to come and see me when Dad was out, but Dad was home when the Doctor came. The doctor only examined my throat and listened to my chest then said, "Marie's throat is very red and that my temperature was high you was right to call me out. Mam told the Doctor that I had changed and that I was depressed. The doctor looked at her and mouthed how much does she know about you? I heard the whispered voice and wondered what he meant. Mam butted in saying "She's a good help to me doctor, she looks after the children, she cooks and she cleans, never needs telling, isn't that right Sam?" Dad said, "Yes she's a rock to the rest of the family, She goes out of her way to please people." The doctor interrupted and said, "How are you coping with your treatment at the hospital?" Tears came into Mam's eyes. I knew this was serious as the doctor patted her hand. Then Mam said in a croaky voice, "Marie is also having nightmares." The doctor said, "Well she is growing up, and moodiness is normal, the nightmares are probably due to the fluctuations in temperature." They both agreed I should have my tonsils out and Dr Nelson said that he would arrange it but I should have antibiotics whilst waiting. My private area was never mentioned and I was too frightened to ask or even tell Mam. I knew I should have told her but I was too scared. Believe me I so wanted to tell the doctor but as Dad never left the room whilst the doctor was there, I couldn't. He just peered at me from over his newspaper eyeballing me as if to warn me, as if to say you keep quiet. Anyway I knew deep inside, Mam already knew what was happening to me and she never even tried to stop it. The doctor said I should start to pick up and feel better and with that he left. Mam saw him to the door muttering as they walked and Dad looked at me and said "Good girl, I will get you something nice when I go out. Mam will make you some jelly which will soothe your throat, maybe some ice cream, that will be nice." I lay down and ignored his words.

After the operation to remove my tonsils, and once my throat healed the sore throats did stop. I did feel a little better and Mam bought me a whip and top. I spent hours trying to perfect the game. The real nightmares, which I had when sleeping, haunted me each and every night they never did stop. I had them for what seamed like years.

A girl from across the road would say our house was haunted and that before we moved in a body was found under the floorboards. I was so scared because weird things did happen over the years so I had no reason to disbelieve her.

Then a second nightmare began, with a severed head hanging on a hook on the back of the bedroom door. It was the head of a woman with long brown scraggy hair, which fell into long curls. It looked like it was matted together with blood. She had her tongue hanging out, long and purple in colour. Her neck looked twisted and her bulging brown eyes were open wide as she stared at me every time I went to bed. She looked terrified, and I was, terrified. I told Mam and she laughed and said it was probably something I had seen on the television, but I never watched horror films then she said all children let their minds play games. The same nightmare happened several times a week. *Who was she, why was she in my room, why did no one else see her, what did she want with me?* I took the dressing gowns off the door hook, thinking it could have been shadows playing tricks but the head still swung from side to side, staring menacingly at me. So every night I started to dread bedtime. Every day I dreaded being alone in the house with Dad and when Mam and Dad were both out, I was left alone with James who would beat me up at every given opportunity. He often taunted whilst hitting me, "Favourite, Daddy's little favourite." His voice was angry and nasty. Yes Dad did give me lots of attention I grant you that, but not for the right reasons and if James knew about my abuse things would be different if only we could have shared with each other how we felt. I would sooner Dad gave his attention to someone else. I never knew whom to turn to, as I was all alone, living in a busy house with seven children, a Mam and a Dad, but living a sole lonely existence, living and dreaming a nightmare.

One day my head was knocked so hard against the wall with my hair being pulled by James, that I fell to the floor and I was semi conscious. When James finally left the hallway I managed to get out of the front door without him seeing me, without a coat. I sat behind the bush near the front gate. He knew I was out there and he came out to say come in, I am sorry I won't hit you again but then he shut the door.

It was a freezing night, but I just could not go back inside. I could not take any more as my mind was going crazy with fear of one thing after another. It did not matter if I froze to death because my life was worthless. I was useless at school, with no friends. My brother used to call me thick, although as I think back he called everyone thick but this was I. My state of mind was not good, so calling me names really did hurt me.

I hated my life, I was always being sick and at this point I just wanted to be free. I wanted to be somewhere where there was no illness, no abuse from James, no abuse to James from Dad and no abuse to me from either of them, a place where Mam was well. Maybe I had to be dead for that, I just wanted out. I was praying that I would freeze to death and maybe God could hear me now. Maybe he heard my cries for help, but he never answered my prayers not one of them not at the time anyway.

The frost lay heavy on the ground and the branches of the bushes were white with soft icy crystals. It was a bleak night with the sky dark blue and stars sprinkled all over it, not a cloud in the sky. Only my mind was cloudy. The wind was cutting through my thin jumper and my bare legs had gone numb. My skirt had absorbed the frost so it was wet with my body heat melting the ice beneath me. I felt very, very cold. My bum had frozen to the earth, and I was shivering so much my ribs hurt. My thoughts were in overdrive, and my chills did not matter. I began to plan a way out, in my head, a way of putting an end to my sad pitiful life. But each time my thoughts became almost sinister planning my escape, then another thought of the family, pushed in on it, which would interrupt. Then I would start planning again and again another thought would interrupt. What about the young uns? I loved them so much, and I loved James even though he beat me. I loved Dad even though he raped me often. I had something wrong with me mentally and I thought my mind was going. I cried and held my aching head in my hands thinking please stop these thoughts this is crazy I am crazy. My lot was here and now and I believed my family all loved me, in some strange way. What could I do about my life? I wanted to end its very existence but how would Mam cope without me? I did think about running away but I was not very street-wise and did not know where to run. Oh God how can I escape from my hell here on earth, both my physical and mental torture? What would I gain if I killed myself? The very thought of having no more pain in both mind and body seemed quite tempting. I began to sweat in my anguish. My thoughts were broken as I heard footsteps crunching on the icy pavement my heart almost stopped, as the steps got closer they brought my mind back to here and now.

Mam opened the gate almost touching my feet. How she did not see me or hear my heart pounding against my chest I will never know. I kept silent and out of sight. I watched as she opened the door to go inside then when she closed the front door, I stood up and watched staring at the house wondering what to do, I shuddered with a cold sweat as I brushed the frost off my skirt. I went to the window and saw Mam as she went into the kitchen and I heard her say "Put the kettle on James, where is Marie? Has she gone to bed?" I never heard the reply. I opened the door very slowly and then I crept inside, climbed the stairs in front of me and went straight to my room. I put my dressing gown on, another pair of socks and tried to snuggle into my bed to try to get warm and again it was as if my brain had just shut down, with no more thoughts of suicide, in fact those thoughts never came into my head again.

Strange really I was convinced my life was not going to be a long lived one as I sat outside in the cold. I told no one I was being beat up by James, as I knew if I told about James, he would get more beatings from Dad. He already had his fair share of those and I could not live with the guilt of causing him more pain. Although after hitting my head so hard against the wall I should have said something, it would have made no difference though.

Dad began saying cruel things to me, he called me names and he said I had thunder thighs and that I was putting on weight. "You should go on a diet," he said. "You're getting fat, stop eating sweets and chocolate. You are beginning to look really fat and horrible you should cut down your meals just look at yourself in a mirror." I could not please him whatever I said or did. He said the jobs in the house were done wrong or accused me of not doing them to his satisfaction. I hung out the wet washing either upside down or wrong; I was just a thorn in his side. He would wake Mam up at three in the morning to clean the house even though he knew she was so ill. She in turn got me out of bed and said that we must clean the house before he got up, so there we were cleaning the door frames with a cloth, mopping floors and dusting in the dead of night just to please him. Then I had to go to school with the young' uns in tow. I was tired; exhausted with the pressure I was under.

I would eat my meals then throw them up in the toilet. My weight just went up and up and as I gained weight so I went on diets to try to lose it; some days I would just eat lettuce. Then he would moan at me because I was constipated and say "If you don't eat you won't shit it's as simple as that. I told you that before". The next day Dad would still say I was fatter than the day before. You must be eating too much he would say again and again, I felt so miserable, everything I did was wrong.

CHAPTER TWENTY EIGHT

NORTHERN IRELAND

As the weeks turned into months Mam gradually got worse. She was either in bed or in hospital most of the time and my schoolwork suffered she had the odd good day when she could get about but in general she was too ill.

In the history class the teacher who really did not like me constantly told me off. He shouted in his bilingual tongue "Marie you are talking, day dreaming, coughing, sneezing?" I always seemed to get hiccups in that class, which he said, upset the rest of the girls. Mind you, I have to say it did send some of them into fits of laughter. I spent a lot of my history lesson at a desk in the corridor. He was never happy even when I pretended to be the slightest bit interested which of course I wasn't. I hated history I hated war. I had a German teacher who only taught about Hitler and the Second World War nothing else just the war, which started in 1939 until it ended in 1945. And he taught everything in between including, Neville Chamberlain and Winston Churchill who were Prime Ministers at that time. I really did not like anything to do with wars. I feared them and then I heard from an Irish girl in my class at school who had family in Northern Ireland that Ireland had declared a civil war between the Catholics and the Protestants in Londonderry. Buildings were being set on fire and bombs were killing innocent people. I got mixed up and thought she said London. I knew I had been there on a bus so it was fairly close to home for me. I was terrified and very upset, it really bothered me, I asked my uncle and he said the Irish have been fighting amongst themselves for years even before the big wars, they would flare up on occasions, and that I should not worry. The IRA was involved and the fighting was usually over a table in a meeting room. He also said he could never see an end to it because religion was the cause of all wars and there will always be religion. I remember questioning him, "Why do people fight over God when he is there for everyone?" My uncle said, "Yes I suppose he is but people still fight. They have all split into different denominations some don't like this and some don't like that so they start another church and call themselves a different name. Different colours and different races will always fight; unfortunately it is the way of the world we live in. People just like fighting and the politicians don't help really." I felt better with his explanation I think I had a little more understanding about my history class and began to find an interest in what was being taught which helped my marks improve.

I liked religious education and began to question with the teacher why religion was the cause of most wars. Right through the bible there were wars between one tribe and another. The teacher said "Wars are predicted in the bible but they are manmade not God made and that God made man and gave them a free will to take care of the land and they chose to fight over it. They always have and always will. It's blamed on religion and it is an excuse because everyone wants to be the greatest ruler of all, there is only one ruler and that is God. People are just not turning to God in prayer, they are dividing into many smaller groups and renaming the churches and doing their own thing and it's not working out. There are too many people under one roof so to speak and no unity." I was top of my class at RE. I always had a good understanding of the word of God, the Holy Trinity being God, Jesus and the Holy Spirit all being one. Some of it made sense and some didn't. The stories in the bible were good to read and it contained some history too, so maybe I did like some history but not the history about war.

In English I was not so good though I actually enjoyed the subject. The same teacher Mrs Spencer also taught needlework which I was very good at. I always did well because me Mam was the best teacher of that subject, she taught me so much in needlecraft, knitting, crochet and darning. I even made my own skirt and came top of my class.

Maths, well that was diabolical. I just did not understand any of it because I did not understand the teacher. She would say "Marie you must ask" and I did ask but her explanation went right over my head and the teacher was not nice either. I got told off time and again for falling behind in my maths work but I just could not do it. It was like reading a foreign language to me making that lesson twice as hard; I dreaded the maths class. I was a hopeless case I heard one teacher say.

The RE teacher whom I really liked seemed different towards me she treated me different and wrote to Mam and said I had won a competition for the school not just the class but also the whole school in Religious Education. I liked the subject and paid attention. She said I won a trip with her and asked if I could go to a Scripture Union Weekend, which was an overnight stay in another town, Peterborough. It was run by churches and was just fun and games, and I was to receive an award. I was absolutely astounded when Mam agreed. Dad however said no, she's not going, and to be honest I really did not care if I went or not. But Mam said you are going, I will see to that. Mam even bought me a new outfit from the wishing book. We travelled on a Saturday morning. We had workshops and games until evening dinner then a disco kind of dance in the evening until around 9ish. I slept in a dormitory with other girls my age. I do not remember one single name of the girls I met, all I know is I enjoyed myself for two days. I felt free for a short while, no one else went from my class just my RE teacher and me. The bus picked up at different churches. I did not know anyone apart from the teacher, but I was encouraged to take part in whatever I wanted to. There was no pressure, no moaning, it was up to me. This was my time, my very special time. On the Sunday we were in a great big hall, praying and singing Christian songs. There were people of all ages talking about God, solo singers and young musicians. It was loud and everyone seemed to be happy, clapping and praising God. Then my bubble burst as it was time to leave and I got on the bus with the teacher, who was so kind and lovely. She never questioned any area of my family business but just asked if I enjoyed myself. I smiled and said "I had a wonderful time," she said I should smile more often, as I nearly always looked sad, I was very sad that day because we had to leave and that was that.

Mam and Dad didn't ask any questions about my Christian week-end away. In fact nothing was ever said about it. I was not asked about what I did. Mam and Dad never mentioned it; they did not even look at my certificate and small white bible, which I still have today.

CHAPTER TWENTY-NINE

FIRST BOYFRIEND

It was 1968 I had gained a few friends at this school but not real friends. One girl named Sheila was my closest friend in my class, though I could never tell my secrets to anyone, not even her. I was not as fashionable as my so-called friends, but we hung out together some nights we hung out on street corners on occasion and listened to the radio. I liked Sheila because she was honest and direct but very gobby and fun. She knew what fun was and acted on it. She made me laugh at times when I felt down but she never asked why I was down. She was okay as an only child and her Mam was a single parent. She told me she never knew her Dad and she said that I was so lucky to have a Mam, Dad, brothers and sisters and I must say that I agreed with her.

Sheila wanted to date a lad in our class and she asked if I would double date with this good-looking boy also in our class. Half the school fancied him but I was not interested in lads though I agreed to go for her sake I was not sure why he would want to date me but he did. Sheila said "I will set up a date for you, we'll double up." I was very nervous and was glad we were together for support when all four of us met up. She had been seeing her boyfriend for a while but he always had this other lad with him and they were never alone. She told me she loved him and that as soon as they left school they were going to get engaged. It was a warm evening and we were walking and chatting we walked towards Tilbury woods. Sheila said "I will see you in a while Marie" and left me with this lad Steve. I felt a bit awkward and embarrassed as I had never had a real boyfriend and did not know how I was supposed to act. He talked a lot and the next minute he pushed me to the ground and started kissing me very hard on the mouth. My heart began to beat fast in panic. I had never kissed a boy before and then his hand went straight up under my top. I never wore a bra as Mam said I did not need one, as I had no bust yet, but I did have small bumps. Steve was happy about the fact I had no bra on and he tried to grope around for my nipples. "Bloody hell," I said. "Get off me." I pushed him hard and he said "What's wrong with you? I thought you fancied me; that's what girls do when they fancy me." "Well I don't," I said. "Now leave me alone, I am not like that." He shouted "Marie I didn't mean to frighten you I thought you had done it before, sex I mean, come on." "Your life will not be worth living if my brothers hear about this," I shouted. And all the lads at school knew I had brothers.

I got up and ran through the woods crying, stumbling over tree stumps, not realising how far we had walked. I fell into a ditch full of wet mud which went all over my clothes and I scraped all down one side of my arm but I managed to get myself out and I ran all the way home sobbing. I was very upset and very angry at the same time. I was screaming inside "Fucking idiot you never should have gone." I figured he must have known my secret somehow, my secret, *but how could he? I maybe looked different from other girls though I was ordinary. My thoughts went into overdrive, wondering how he could possibly think I was going to have sex with him.* The next day at school Sheila asked me what happened and when I told her she laughed and said "There is nothing wrong with having sex." I replied, "I am not ready for sex yet and I'm not like you. I will never have sex with a boy because I'm not ready and I don't know Steve very well, it was only our first date shit how can a lad expect sex on a first date."

Word soon got around. I could hear other boys laughing and looking. Steve told other boys we had had a grope in the woods but that's as far as it went because I was frigid. I looked the word up in the dictionary and later when I was 16 another man said the same. I managed however to ignore the torment from the boys at school. I never had another boyfriend whilst I was at school. In fact I never socialised with any boys after that for ages. I only had a few months left at school and then I'd have to go to work so I decided to get on with my life without the interference of boys.

A few weeks later Sheila was crying. She was pregnant; her boy-friend dumped her of course. The boy she loved so much just walked away but her Mam was really lovely and supported her all the way. She managed to hide it well. I was so scared for her but my own circumstances scared me more. She had a baby girl just after we left school and then married a really nice guy who loved her and her baby.

I was being sick a lot, my stomach was getting bigger and I was gaining weight. Dad continued calling me fat. He also said that no boy would ever ask me out because I was so fat. I was 14 and about 9 stone, which was overweight but not obese. I just ignored him and yet the pain I felt from his words was cutting and hurting me so much I began to worry about my weight and started eating just lettuce. It was just on Saturdays then it went to 2 or 3 days a week. Then I became very constipated and he would say "If you don't eat you won't shit you stupid girl, eat this" and he would pile my plate with potatoes and almost force me to eat. Then I would go out to be sick, I just could not win.

Linda said her Mam told her she could not be a friend with me any-more as I was a bad influence on her and that she thought my family was rough. I said "But we have been friends all through school, what do you have that makes you think you are better than me?" My best friend was saying goodbye. She was no better than me. In fact I was a good girl because I had no interest in sex due to my special secret. She was the one who ended up pregnant at 16 again I felt sorry for her before she fell pregnant the boys Mother asked if I would take him out as their relationship was getting too serious we went to the pictures and that was all I did not fancy him and he loved my friend what did his Mother want me to do we were just mates on the street.

Linda did marry him they had their baby and I think they were happy together the families just had to be happy for them.

CHAPTER THIRTY

NO DAD NO

As the weeks followed Dad never asked me to join him, until one Sunday afternoon in March, when Mam was very ill, lying on the sofa in the front room, with the flickering warmth of the fire in the grate. Dad came home from the pub and said "Upstairs Marie." I followed him upstairs and he collapsed on the bed as I stood at the door. When he said "Come here, I need you today lock the door Marie" I wanted to be sick on the floor right in front of him. I looked at him right in the eyes and I said "No Dad no! I will not come to you today or any other day, it's wrong I was holding my head and was not really conscious of what I was saying it just blurted out. "I will tell the police if you ever touch me again, I really mean it, enough is enough. You make me sick and I hate you, I hate what you have done to me and I hate you for being my Dad you are supposed to be my Dad." I slammed the door shut. I was petrified, shaking, crying and was ready to run away. I did not know where I would run to but I would definitely have to leave and never come home again. We had looked at each other straight in the eyes and he did not say a word, absolutely nothing came from his mouth. I was trembling with fear. I ran down the stairs, put my coat on and ran out the house down the path through the gate where I was physically sick, I wiped my mouth and ran until I could hardly breath I was so out of breath.

I slowed down and walked for what seemed to be miles around and around the streets, not daring to go home. I did not know what to do or what to expect even if I were to go back home. I walked to the fields where I went with the young uns where the buttercups and daisies bloomed and the trickling brook ran down the hill. I stood in that field alone, with no one to turn to. I shouted "God are you there? Why, why aren't you helping me? You are supposed to love all people. Why are you ignoring me? Why haven't you answered my prayers?" I fell to my knees in the field and I prayed to God once more.

"If you do not answer my prayer this time I promise you I will never pray again. I do not know what to do. Do I go home or run away? I made a decision to say no to Dad but now what, tell me God, now what? Who can help me? I feel so helpless, so useless I hate myself, I hate my Dad."

"Please help me, please help me." I was crying uncontrollable and I hurt so much.

"I have always believed in you and for what?" I was actually screaming at God. "Come on show yourself; do you really exist? Or are you just another story in a book like Dad said? Please don't let him be right I trusted you, you know everything you know all my darkest secrets. What's the point in me telling you if you cannot help me?"

I had no money, no clothes, and nowhere to go. No one would ever believe me even if I told them. And Mam, what would happen to her? She could die, and my precious June and Carol what would happen to them and Robert where would he go? Please God help me. Who would love and take care of them? I would have to go home; if there were any trouble I would tell Mam everything. I knew she knew about my secret anyway really, she knew what was happening with Dad and chose to do nothing about it, as she had sent me to him on several occasions in the past, Why God, Why did she do that?

I was in terrible pain with my stomach and felt as though my inside was going to drop out. My head was throbbing as I had been hitting it with my hands, out of sheer frustration.

I was in a daze walking around the field until my steps took me back home. A man stopped and asked if I was all right. I do not remember my response because I was sobbing from deep within. I just walked for what seemed like hours, although I was only a few miles away from home.

After reaching the front door I stood staring at it for a while, then slowly opened it. I saw Robert and asked where Dad was. "He's in the kitchen, why are you in trouble? He's in a good mood. He just got up and gave me a chocolate bar; he doesn't seem that mad with you." "What do you mean, what do you know Robert?" I ranted at him "What do you know?" but he ran off shouting "Marie has gone mad. Mam she is all red and has been crying."

Dad came through to me and said, "What is the matter with you has someone upset you?" He stroked my shoulder. "As if you care," I said. He walked off into the kitchen, and then Mam said in almost a whisper "You will be all right Marie come and sit with me a while."

Mam was in the living room laying on the bed dad had brought downstairs for her, I sat on the bed at the side of her and I explained I had very bad pains in my stomach and I had brown stuff in my pants not much but it was there. She smiled at me and said, "Well you are that age, and it's your time. I have been expecting this day. Yer Dad will," and then she stopped. "Take a pain killer, Aspirin and let me know what happens." I said, "Mam are you going to die? You are getting worse aren't you? You hardly get out of bed anymore". She said, "I am not going anywhere. I will always be here with you children. Please stay with me for a while." So I lay alongside her and I felt comfortable, warm and safe for the first time in a very long time.

Sure enough the next day I had my first period. I went to see Mam who said, "Now you need to keep clean and always keep some sanitary towels in the house hide them so the boys don't see them. When the van comes on the street I will go with you to the van to buy some. But you will have to deal with it; you're a woman now it's your job to check yourself. That's why you've put on some weight, no other reason." She had tears in her eyes as she spoke. "I will tell your Dad when he gets home and he will leave you alone". I did not click at that point what Mam had said (I would tell him to leave you alone) You are now at risk of getting pregnant so you must take care of yourself and no playing those silly games with the boys when you are on a period you attract the boy and you can get pregnant. We used to play spin the bottle and when it landed on you, you had a forfeit and had to show a boy or girl depending on who it landed on a part of your covered body either your thigh or a breast if you were brave enough, and sometimes they might have a quick grope, but I never agreed to those things but Mam caught two of them having a grope one night not me but she assumed we all did it.

Your brothers need never know when you are on your period. It's private be careful not to leave anything lying around." I gave her a look I admit I did not ever know she if it was her period but there was often blood on her clothes and she was always washing towels out that she had slept on, I now know it was the radiotherapy the burning of her cancer which caused her to bleed so heavy as she had an hysterectomy years before and therefore did not have periods anymore and when she did Mam could not afford Sanitary towels and use cut up sheets because she bled very heavy and soaked them in a bucket in the kitchen everyone knew I'm sure, secondly she said I could get pregnant whilst on a period, I wonder if she really knew anything about sex education, I remember considering a conversation about it but felt it was not my place it just was not spoken about.

I was nearly 15 when my periods began. The rest of my school friends started theirs much earlier. Although at the time I thought there was there something wrong with me, or rather I thought I might have been damaged inside, through what he had done to me, I spoke to Sheila and she explained what was going on and told me she had a period at 13 that is the reason she missed so much PE at school, it's funny really how some things make sense when they are explained anyway I felt better after that.

CHAPTER THIRTY ONE

SCARS

Mam wanted to show me how her illness had progressed. She showed me her stomach, it was like a road map full of scars and it looked really sore and red raw. She said, "I hope it has not upset you too much Marie, I just want to help you to understand." I nodded, meaning I was not upset. I had a lump in my throat and struggled to speak. She never knew just how much it had affected me but like my other secrets it got buried deep inside. My heart was already heavy with what I was already hiding from everyone and now this. As soon as I was well enough I helped even more. I shovelled coal from outside in the coalbunker. We had 4 buckets and I filled them all every day. I would run down to the shops in my school dinner hour to fetch something for Dad's dinner in the evening which meant I did not have time to get anything to eat. Mam always read a magazine called the Detective, so that was on my list of things I had to buy from the shops.

On the days Mam was not well I had to take the day off school. This was nearly always on a Monday. I knew each Monday when it was bad weather or Mam was too ill to set the washing machine up as it was a rented twin tub it had to be dragged from the other side of the kitchen, then filled up, it was not very big and washing took most of the day, so I had to take the washing to the launderette in the pram. The launderette was always full of old women chatting and they even took sandwiches to eat. I used to think it was an outing for them, a kind of a gossip group catching up on all the news from each different street. I always had to wait my turn for the dryers and sometimes other would push in front because I was a child I had to have respect. Washing machines lined one side of the washhouse and dryers lined the other side with a red box of Daz wash powder on each washer with the exception of a few, which had a blue Surf box on top. There were coloured plastic baskets scattered all around the floor. The women would always interfere and say, "Don't push all that in their deary, use one of the big machines or else you'll break them." Then another woman said, "We won't have any machines to do our washing in and you should leave that mucky pram outside." I tried to ignore them, and carried on and I couldn't do as they asked anyway as my washing was not in a bag and I was not going to carry dirty socks, knickers and goodness knows what else it in my arms so I ignored them and pushed the pram right by them inside. I had no choice which machine I used because I hadn't enough money for the large machine, and I would not be able to dry it, and as it was always raining when this chore had to be done, I just went ahead and pushed it all in. The women just chuntered "Cheeky little madam, got no manners now' a days, and why aren't you at school anyway?" *I thought, "What's it got to do with you nosey cows."* I looked around and said in a loud tone, "Me Mam's ill and I have to do it and that's that." Then I sat down and said no more. The women just moaned on between themselves. Even now I have a phobia of launderettes. The thought of my washing machine breaking down for more than a week laid on my mind for years to come. The smell in the launderette was nauseating, dirty clothes; sometimes damp mouldy smells, mingling with the smell of clean clothes, soap and food. The women who didn't take sandwiches bought chips from the chip shop next door, probably a day out for some of them, a picnic and a gossip.

I followed Mam's instructions to the letter and was only allowed to play when I had done my chores. Mam's visits to the neighbours got fewer and I was left with all the chores and children. They were too young to do anything to help but at least now they were all at school and I had to go and collect two of them at 3.00 and Robert at 3.15. I had to rush up to school and run back so I did not see the teachers and girls from my class. If I did they would shout "Bunking off again Marie? Ooh look at the under age Mam." I ran dragging Robert behind me, they taunted me and called my family because there were so many of us. I wanted to punch them, smash their heads in, but I held it together my Mam was too ill for me to cause any bother they were not worth it.

I missed school a lot to look after the home, Mam, or the young uns and I really liked school. I enjoyed the learning although I was not the brightest button in the tin. I was of average intelligence but I did try. Given the chance and maybe in a different life I believe I could have done much more with my brain but even at school I was not allowed to be myself. It was an all girls' school and some of the girls were not happy about me being in their class, mainly because I was from a big family, even though some of the others also came from fairly big families. They did not seem to get ridiculed and picked on like I did. This was probably because I was never without a child attached to me and because one of us always had nits, which everyone else knew about because we all had to queue up to see the school nit nurse. She would soak our hair through with a horrible sticky stuff, which smelt vile, everyone new when your head was drenched in solution.

I always had to leave school 15 minutes early to collect the young uns from class as they finished school before I did. I could not stay and socialise with the girls at the school gates, which was what they all did, not that they wanted me to. Maybe if I made an effort they might have liked me.

One Wednesday after school I was a little late, as I had stayed behind for scripture union with a teacher. There were only five of us and it was only half an hour long, extra study about the bible. I liked the quietness of the classroom it was a little piece of me time and I enjoyed Theology that is why I stayed. After it finished I walked to the gate. There was a crowd of girls standing talking. One of them said, "Here's that freak that can't come and hang out because her Mam makes her do everything." I did not give in to my emotions; it was not the right time to get upset but I knew I had to walk through them. One girl pushed me as I passed, so I reached out, grabbed her long brown hair and pulled her to the ground and gave her a good punch. The others were shouting "Scrap, scrap," whilst I was punching her. I was saying you can call me, but don't ever call my mam. You know nothing about my mam. Then I kicked her in

136

the stomach and walked away saying "Anyone else?" They all went to her aid and ignored me; I heard one say "Bloody hell where did that come from feisty little sod isn't she." I just went straight home looking over my shoulder at intervals.

I could not keep a friend because my life was so full of other stuff. There were jobs to do, a Dad who did not want me to have friends. The schools were set around a big playing field, the boys one side and the girls the other and the senior school on the other side. A little like a compass, north, south, east and west and the nursery was attached to the end of my block. I felt I was losing my childhood and I quickly became withdrawn. I was growing up too fast for the other kids in school to understand; even the teachers didn't understand the traumas in my life. They were always interested in my bruises but when I said James did them when we were fighting, which was partly true, in between the kicking I got from a couple of bullies in school, it was not pursued by the teachers. It was soon forgotten about and the subject was always dropped.

The next day I went into school wondering what was in store for me, the girl who was the bully was not in my class but the girl I hit was. She just looked down at her desk and said nothing. It was very quiet all that day. At playtime I went to the toilet block in the playground and there they were. Four girls from the previous night stood smoking one cigarette between them. I walked by with my head down, none of them spoke to me about the night before but I was nervous and carried on walking. All of a sudden they put the cigarette in my hand and said "Smoke it freak," pushing my arm towards my face, "Go on have a drag." I feared for my safety so I put the cigarette to my mouth. They all went to a toilet in silence, four toilet cubicles in a row. A teacher walked in, got me by the scruff of my neck and took me to see the head mistress cigarette still in hand.

I was set up why did I fall for it? The head mistress gave me one cane across the hand, which held the cigarette and said, "Go." It stung like mad but I did not cry I had had worse. I learnt another lesson that day. How was I going to survive the little time I had left at school and why isn't God helping me again when I need him? I decided I had to make a friend, someone in the know. That's when I began hanging around with Sheila who was popular with all the girls and boys for that matter she did turn out to be a friend to me. I told her some of my problems about Mam being ill. The girl who I had fought with sent her friend Cheryl over to me in the playground. She gave me a pasting, knocking me to the floor. The next day during PE the teacher noticed I was badly bruised and whisked me to the heads office. She was accusing my Dad of hitting me, so I had to tell the truth that it was Cheryl who had hit me the previous day. She questioned Cheryl and nothing more was said about the matter. I survived with no more beatings from the girls, they just ignored me and no one chose me for their team when sides were picked for team sports and that was okay by me, I never liked sports anyway, and I just used to run around the hockey pitch on my own. I was more than happy with my own thoughts.

CHAPTER THIRTY-TWO

THE DEATH OF ME MAM

On the 2nd April 1969 at 8 am Dad said "I need you to stay off school today Marie." My heart sunk as I thought he had an ulterior motive, though he said nothing. I said, "No Dad I want to go to school," so he said, "Ok you go to school." When I got home at lunchtime I was washing the pots in the kitchen after I had had a sandwich for lunch. Dad came behind me and touched my shoulder. I shuddered and pulled away but he said, "Marie you need to know your mother is very ill I mean very ill." I was listening in silence then he said " Marie do you understand what I am trying to say, I mean it could be today or tomorrow." I cried and said, "What do you mean?" He said "She is going to die Marie, please do not go to school this afternoon you need to stay with her she needs you with her she is frightened Marie. I want you to stay with her Please Marie just sit with her, she needs someone here all the time she has asked for you now go to her leave the pots I will bring you in a drink it's warm in there, sit with her, hold her hand."

The tears began to flow with the reality of my worst nightmare. He left me alone in the kitchen and went upstairs. I gained composure and went and sat with Mam I felt confused, what can I say to her; I just did not know what to say, so I told her I loved her and held her hand like Dad had said. She was asleep most of the time but she looked at me with half open eyes surrounded with dark circles. She looked very pale and her skin was a creamy yellow not one wrinkle on her face, she whispered my name a few times then stopped. I held her hand for hours in an unbroken silence just Mam's slow soft breathing until her time was nearing the end then she began to gasp for pockets of air hanging onto the little life she had left. Her dying words in a faint whisper were, "Look after the young ones and don't let him send you into a home all stay together you are their Mam now you will cope Marie. I love you Marie." I could just make out her faint words. I hugged her sobbing holding back my tears for fear of upsetting her. She took a last gasp and died. Mam died at 5 minutes past 8. I had not noticed Dad in the room he was stood near the door, "Why didn't you come over Dad". "Because this was important for you Marie I had my time this morning we said good-bye this morning". I held onto her hand looking at her peaceful face she was gone I know and free from pain but in my selfish thoughts I did not want her to go nor did I want to leave her.

Dad pulled me away and said, "She's gone Marie she's gone." James was upstairs putting a new window in the bathroom, which had been cracked with a ball; he kept busy whilst Mam was dying. George shouted upstairs "Stop James," and all went silent. James knew but he could not face being in the same room. Dad then sent me around to a neighbour's house, where Robert, June and Carol were watching television. June came over to me and asked if I was crying. I said, "Yes" and was just about to say Mam had died when the neighbour said, "Come on now the young ones don't need to know, they will know soon enough." Then she said, "Now no more tears now, stop crying, you will upset everyone else, come and have a drink in the kitchen." I went into the kitchen where I was told not to cry. I wanted to cry so much with the fear I held inside of the future without Mam. I needed her, why couldn't I cry for goodness sake? My Mam had just died not ten minutes ago. The neighbour said that I had to be strong for the young ones as I would be their Mam now. They needed me as they were still babies and I was all grown up. "I know," I said and gave a big sob, the neighbour interrupted "But you have to be Mam to them young ones, so dry your eyes, and say nothing tonight. Leave it to the aunts to tell them."

I did as I was told and sat staring at the television showing no emotion, not registering what was on the TV. I had June sitting on one knee and Carol on the other. Robert sat on the floor each of them munching on a biscuit, Mrs Johnson brought me in a cup of tea "Drink this Marie it will do you good".

Robert had guessed something was not right and sat quiet he was a little older at 8 and no more was said. When we arrived home late on that Wednesday night. The young ones went straight to bed bypassing the front room where Mam lay and Dad was making arrangements with my older brother. George said "Marie put the kettle on and make some tea for us all, you have no need to come in here." Mam's friend Eileen came around and dressed Mam putting cotton wool into her nose, and other parts of her anatomy. They call that dressing. "Marie wash up the cups before you go to bed." I went into the room to catch a last glimpse of me Mam I scurried around collecting cups I rinsed them out and went up to bed hoping it was just another nightmare. I never prayed that night, and I never slept. I got up for a wee and there at the top of the stairs stood me Mam in her nightgown "Ah Mam you made me jump". I sighed a sigh of relief thinking I had dreamed all happenings of the evening so I went back to bed and must have slept until morning.

When I woke up I was startled by Dad in the room he sat beside me, "Marie we have got to pull together I am not sure how we are to cope with all this". The nightmare was as true as true could be, Mam was dead, so who did I see?

The days were passing, somehow I had to survive, Dad did not have time for any of us so I cooked and looked after the young uns. The night before the funeral I saw Mam again large as life at the top of the stairs just like when I saw her on the night of her death. She looked at me with a gentle loving look, dressed in a white cotton nightgown. I told my aunt the next day and she said she saw her too in her house, and that she was saying goodbye and that she would look down on us and guide us in the best way she could. The words I was hearing were wonderful. I wondered at that point how my life would pan out now.

After the funeral I went back to school. My form teacher had had it in for me for a while now for no real reason.

The school had changed into a comprehensive school during the last year and so there were also boys in our class. It was a horrible for the teachers as they had only ever taught girls and the boys' teachers had only ever taught boys so no one really knew how to cope with the mixed sex classes. The boys got severely punished when they did wrong. I often heard the strap whizzing down on a boy's backside and the screaming from a classroom, or the slipper, or the cane, which was about 18 inches long and very thin and it stung like hell. All these things were meant to be a deterrent for naughty or mischievous kids. The girls only had the cane, which was not used that often. We now had a male head teacher who I thought was alright but the deputy head was a woman who was an absolute cow who just did not like children how can that be? Every time I saw her she was scolding a child for something, tidy yourself up girl sort your hair out fasten your shoelace pull that skirt down it is far too short, lots of girls including myself would roll the waistband over and over to shorten the length, she even shouted down the corridors less chatting go to your lessons even if we had none to go to.

I had had a lot of time off in recent years because of Mam's illness and this put me a long way behind the kids in my class. I struggled with my schoolwork, which didn't help things. One particular day the lads in my class were all acting up and the girls just giggled at their antics, as you did with a class of adolescent 14 year old kids. Each desk sat two and they were in rows. It was two girls then two boys and the boys were always last to come into class. Some of the girls had put drawing pins on the lad's seats, so when they sat down they got a prick in the backside. The teacher was getting very angry and was not being heard by the class so she banged a hand brush on the front of my desk to try and quieten everyone down. The bristle part flew off right to the back of the room creating hysterical laughter. It was hilarious. The teacher's face went ashen; the anger brought her to my desk for some reason and she lashed out hitting me right across the side of my face knocking me off my chair. The kids all went silent, as she tried to help me up. I pushed her off me and said "You cow, you bloody cow, how dare you fucking hit me, you cow, it was the whole bloody class not just me." Whilst holding my face I ran out of the classroom and out of the school gates and around the block wondering what I should do. I wandered the streets for the rest of the afternoon. I dare not go home and I dare not go back to school.

I never said a word at home that teatime. The following day I walked into the playground to the girl I had made a friend of and I was surrounded by a crowd of boys and girls from all other classes saying I was in big trouble and they didn't know how I dare come back to school, after swearing at a teacher the way I did. The headmaster came over and said "Break it up, what's going on here?" Everyone dispersed leaving me face to face with him. I looked him right in the eye and said "What?" He asked if I was all right. I think my face must have gone white as I felt the blood drain from it. He turned his back and walked away, some of the crowd moved back in, admiring my braveness when the bell rang and we all went back to class.

When I arrived in class my form teacher was not there instead there was a male teacher. He said very calmly "Marie headmaster's office now." I swallowed hard and got up from my chair. It felt as though everyone was staring at me; I could feel their eyes on me. When I reached the headmasters office I was offered a drink and was told to sit down. The Cow walked through the door slowly tapping the cane onto her other hand. She put the cane down on a table away from where we were sitting. My thoughts were of running away. Why did they give me a drink? Why was I about to get the cane? Nothing was making any sense to me. There were three teachers in the room, one was my RE teacher Miss Turner, one was my English teacher Mrs Spencer and the other was the Cow Miss Aldridge.

They all took a seat and said between them "What are we going to do with you?" The RE teacher said "We understand your Mam has just died?" I said "Yes, last week." "So how do you feel?" the Cow said. I wanted to say how do you think I feel you stupid cow it's me Mam, but I held back and shrugged my shoulders. Mrs Spencer took my hand and said, "It's ok to be upset." I told her no I am not allowed to be upset because I have to stay strong for the young uns. They all looked at each other and shook their heads. The Cow said, "Oh but you must cry if you need to, my dear, you cannot bottle something like this up." I saw softness in her face, which I had never seen before. I thought perhaps she was human after all. I said "No I am not allowed to cry Dad said I have to be strong. "Right," the Cow said. "We will have to understand but we are all here for you if you need someone to talk to." I thought yeah right like I am going to come to you all upset. I knew deep inside that would never happen because of my secret. I was worried that if one thing came out my secret might.

It was about a week since me Mam's funeral and I went to school one day to find my own form teacher at the front of the class. She really looked ill; she said, "Come in Marie take your seat." The class was surprisingly quiet and then Mrs McGowan began the lesson. A little way through the morning she said "I have an award to give out this morning for the essays which were handed in before I was off. I read them all and some were better than others and research had been done on some and not on others. I had to pick out the best, which was Marie's; can you come to the front of the class Marie?" I stood up and walked slowly to the front and she handed me a huge chocolate Easter egg. I said, "Thank you, I thought I might have had an apology first," and I dropped it at her feet. The smash of the chocolate egg was seen and heard by everyone in the classroom. The silence was chilling, not a single breath could be heard. She looked at me and said in a very soft voice, "I have to understand that you did that because your Mam has just died. Go back to your seat Marie," and without a word I moved back to my seat. She picked up the egg and took it to the storeroom. The kids just stared at me in amazement. That was the turning point at school and no one picked on me ever again. All of a sudden I had friends, if that is what you call them. I was admired for standing up for myself but I hated myself for the way I was changing, I knew it was not for the better. Soon after the incident with the Easter egg Mrs McGowan died of cancer just like my Mam but I was still without emotion.

At the age of 15 after Mam died, my life took another turn. My endurance in that year was stronger than ever. I found some inner strength to persevere with the life, which was planned out for me. My day started getting the young uns ready for school then myself, then breakfast when we had some. I did a drop off walk to school. Luckily all the schools were around the circle but nevertheless a task in itself. The head teacher arranged my school around the young uns, I first dropped Robert and June off at infant school, then I took

Carol to nursery and I went on to do my day at secondary school. At 3.00 I had to collect June from infant school to sit in my class colouring for 30 minutes whilst I finished my lesson. I thought it was good that the teachers allowed this. She was always a very good girl, right up to when the bell rang at 3.30. June and I would leave school to collect Carol from nursery who was always the last there because of our situation. The nursery helper stayed behind until we collected her, then we had the walk home which took us about half an hour as the girls were slow walkers and tired. Robert had left school, it was arranged that he would go home with a friend, so he was sorted. When we got home I cooked tea for us all including James when he was at home he worked as an apprentice carpenter.

Some time after I walked in the house to hear Carol screaming. As I ran upstairs all I could hear was Dad shouting open yer bloody legs, yer mardy arse. Alarm bells started to ring in my head. I shouted "Oh my God what are you doing?" as I burst into his bedroom. Carol was lying on the bed with no knickers on and her dress up over her head. I ran at him almost pushing him over, "What are you doing?" I shouted, Dad replied, "It's not what it looks like Marie." I shouted to him "If you ever touch any of my sisters I promise I will kill you when you are sleeping, I will stab you and sod the consequences you perverted bastard, I mean it Dad, I really mean it." He shouted, "Tell your sister Carol, tell her!" He slapped her leg, "For God's sake tell her what I was doing." She was crying too much to speak, and I know what I saw. He had the Vaseline pot on the bed and his hand was touching her private part that's what I could see.

The memories came flooding back in torrents, which engulfed me for a while. He said "Look she is sore, you do it then she needs some cream putting on her. Marie I never touched her." I could see that Carol was very sore down there but I wanted to know why? She flung her arms up to my neck and said "Marie please don't ever leave me." "Of course I won't ever leave you I promise." As I walked out of the room with Carol I turned to him and said, "You better leave her alone, never touch her again I will kill you, I will kill you do you hear?" My anger was that of someone who could have stabbed him right there and then had I had a knife handy. I took her to our room

145

and just cradled her in my arms calming her and at the same time calming myself. I whispered to her "Never ever go to Dad with private things always ask me, do you hear me?" She stopped sobbing and nodded to agree; she nestled her head into my chest and cried "I want me Mam is she coming back Marie?" Then June came in, climbed onto my knee nudging Carol to one side, I told them both "Never go to Dad on your own, tell me everything I am your Mam now and you can tell me anything at all, I will take care of you." June said "Don't Dad love us anymore?" I said "Yes of course he does but he's going through a hard time at the moment, but just you both remember I will always be here for you." Then I began crying inside, giving out a little deep breath to hide my own fear. My mind was speaking with no words, Mam what have you left me with? How can I stop him hurting my sisters? Why did you die? I had so many unanswered questions and I felt so alone with my fear. I vowed to myself that I would kill him if I ever found out he had abused my sisters, I knew that I would be sent to prison if I killed him but I didn't care about that he had left me alone for some months now was he abusing them instead?

We rarely saw Dad as he was either working or down the pub. He was doing the best he could to keep a meal on the table but I cleaned, washed, ironed, cooked, and never having any time for myself. So long as the young uns were safe, that's all I cared about. I had made Mam a promise on her dying words; I promised to take care of them until they were old enough to take care of themselves and I believe I did just that. I was the young uns substitute Mam but I never believed that anyone could take the place of yer Mam or do a good job like Mam, I believe, Mam's are special, a bond between mother and child should never be broken in our case it was different she had been taken away for ever and she was not coming back to help or advise. I did the best I could and I loved my sisters just like any Mam. All I wanted to do was to protect them and keep them safe from harm but being so young myself I had a limited capability and they did not always listen to me. Our aunt who lived just up the road played a large part in our growing up, especially the young uns but I was their rock at home they came to me about most things.

CHAPTER THIRTY THREE

MY SIXTEENTH BIRTHDAY

It was 1970 Mam had been dead a year and 1 month. I had bought a new dress as Dad said he had planned a party for my 16th birthday, it was at my aunt's pub in Leicester, Dad had invited other members of the family to celebrate with us. My uncle provided the music entertainment; he played the piano and everyone was singing and dancing, a good time was being had by all and it was nice to see the family a year on from Mam's death it had been a hard year for us all.

I was drinking soft drinks all night but by the end of the evening I was so drunk I could hardly stand. I found out that Dad was lacing my soft drinks with spirits but I did not know this. All the way home I felt so ill, everything was spinning around so fast and I felt as though I would pass out. I had been sick all down my dress; it was all over my face and in my long hair. When we got home Dad held my head with my hair over the kitchen sink as I continued to vomit, then he said "That will teach you to get drunk you sod, don't let me ever see you drunk again, do you hear me? I am not having it." He shook my head hard, which sent me so dizzy I could hardly stand up. "Do you understand?" I mumbled something whilst almost choking on my own vomit.

He began undoing the front buttons to my dress. The dress fell to the floor and he stared at my body as he bent down to pick up my dress. I was slouched hanging onto the draining board dressed only in my bra and pants. He pushed me to one side and started rinsing my dress under the tap after forcing my vomit down the plughole with his own fingers and hot running water, the site of him doing that only made me vomit more. He then threw my wet dress in to the washing machine. I started crying partly because of the alcohol and the fact I felt very ill but mainly because I was terrified what would happen next as I was not in any fit state to fight him off. He took my arm and led me upstairs and he pushed me through the bedroom door. I fell not quite knowing where I was but I had landed on my own bed somehow but not the right way up. I looked through very blurry eyes as Dad stared into my face, as the venomous words came from his mouth. "Sleep it off, you're a disgrace." He walked out. I thought he may have had an ulterior motive but I do not remember anything else of that night.

The next morning Dad came into my room and opened all the windows. He shouted, " How are you this morning come on get out of bed, the house needs cleaning." I turned over and said, "Later." He grabbed the blankets and yanked them off the bed and said, "This will teach you to get drunk girl, now get up."

"I don't understand how I got drunk as I was on orange juice I feel so ill! He smirked "I did it to teach you not to drink again."

"Oh that was not fare nor was it funny you make me sick."

I knew everyone else would still be sleeping so it was easier to get up than to argue with him and I knew he would be going to the pub later so I could rest then.

I did not drank very little alcohol again until I was 19 years old, so maybe his little trick did work though I was not a big fan anyway and I always felt I needed to be on my guard, as I always felt insecure in the house.

I started going to pubs when I was 17 years old with people from work but only drank orange juice. Dad always waited up for me to come home and often he was sitting in front of the fire drunk. If he heard me creeping in the door he would shout, "It's late, where have you been? Have you been with boys? They are all only after one thing, the pubs have been shut for hours, where have you been." He followed that with "Marie the pots need washing before you go to bed". If it wasn't the pots it was something else that needed doing.

Sometime later I began to focus on my life again and as I sat on my bed I realised I was sitting in a bedroom not much better than a pigsty. In fact looking back a pigsty was probably cleaner. I moved my bed to the middle of the room as the bedroom was in desperate need of a good clean and as there was not much room to move furniture about, it was a matter of dragging the bed across the lino and climbing back over it to clean underneath. I know I was aware that I would find dirt and dust under my bed but I was not prepared for what came next. In the corner was a huge spider's web quite thick almost like a knitted grey blanket attached to two walls from corner to corner almost in a perfect triangle. I hastily searched for the spider as I imagined it to be as big as a tarantula with the size of the web. I was worrying it would raise its head at any moment and whilst I was not particularly scared of spiders I imagined this one to be big so I was very wary and poked and prodded a tee shirt with a knitting needle which I found that was almost invisible against the brown lino. As I looked further I could see a spider was dried up and lying dead next to a single sock of mine. This one although dried up did not look as if it could have been capable of weaving such a thick web so I carried on looking. I had hoped that was the one, but I cautiously picked things up and shook them whilst my mind was thinking of an escape plan should huge spider run out. The dust was thick with numerous books and odd things I had not missed or seen in month's maybe years. I don't remember the last time I cleaned under my bed and Mam had died over a year ago now, so the house was somewhat neglected. Not that Mam cleaned it often but she did tell me what needed cleaning and told me when to do it. Now no one seemed to bother much anymore about the bedrooms, I cleaned the downstairs every week because that was Dad's orders along with the bathroom but my bedroom did get ignored.

I could not find another spider and went for the vacuum. As I was vacuuming the floor with the hose I noticed something in the web. I jumped back thinking it moved and it was the spider but it was me that sucked a little of the web causing it to quiver. I bent down to see what was intriguing me so much and the shape of a small figure appeared in the web, it was standing in the corner with the web entwined with thick lacy silk was me Mam from my perfect imaginary family, which lived in the dolls house, I fell to my knees and wept as I thought of my real Mam dying and leaving me to get on with things. I carefully lifted the figure out of the web; I brushed off the dust and cupped it in my hands as I actually thanked the spider for protecting it for me.

A song came on the radio 'Reflections of My Life' by Marmalade. I sobbed and yelled inside my head still afraid to let my emotions go, as I listened to the words; *take me back to my old home, reflections of my life.* Why oh why did you take me Mam God? It was not her time to die, she was only 44 years old so why? How will I cope? At 16 I felt I was running the house, what with Dad's drinking and James lashing out all the time. I was always a servant but somehow became a slave to the home. The young uns need a Mam not me, are you listening God? I am only a kid myself, they need a Mam, I hate you God, I hate you for leaving me here with him, and he's always drunk. Why didn't you take me years ago when I asked? Me Mam is dead and I need her so much, the young uns need her. I cried inside without tears until my ribs ached, then I heard the front door slam and quickly rubbed my face thinking even without tears the evidence of crying would be visible. I carried on sucking up the spider's web, which had protected my little figure all these years. My thoughts travelled back to the days of my dolls house and there I was lost in time cleaning and thinking in a world of my own.

Dad appeared at the door and said, "Are you alright?" I did not look at him but did answer him "Yes, why?" He said "You know things will get better and will settle down, I will change, we will go out this weekend I will take you all to a park and show you where I met your Mam and the park where I took her courting." I said, "Yes that would be nice."

I carried on cleaning pushing my thoughts deep down within my soul where my pain and secrets were all safe, where they could not hurt me anymore. I put the figure of me Mam in a gap in the floorboards, it was gone now forever and I did not think about the dolls house or my perfect family or my abuse or God again, I never wanted the memories to come into my mind ever again so it was best that they should be buried. I thought they were never to emerge again, forever lost in eternity, until years later when the volcano erupted.

Dad did get a picnic ready that weekend and we all bundled into the car and drove to Retford where he took us all to see an uncle who we'd never seen before. There was a little old man sat in the chair near the window, the house was smelly uncared for and old just like the man who sat there. Dad told him about me Mam and we left. Dad showed us the army barracks where he met Mam and then we all went on the park and as we all stood on a bridge that went over a stream Dad took a photograph of us and said "You look like the Von Trapp family from the Sound of Music film." Dad did not know but it was my favourite film in the whole world as it was one that Mam saw 9 times in her final years and she took me with her 3 times. Mam and I had some very special moments together in her final years but I was not to know she was leaving me at the time.

Looking back I know that I was very lucky in one respect because Robert, June and Carol all missed out, as they did not grow up with a Mam. At least I had almost 15 years with her. They missed out more than anyone could imagine and now I was their Mam and would always be there for them. I know I could never replace our Mam but at least I could protect them from Dad, unlike me own Mam who sent me to him. He will never touch them, not while ever I have breath and I believe I was kept alive by God in my despair to protect them the best I could. But God was not part of my life anymore at this time; he died with Mam that was the final straw for my relationship with God.

Whenever I was at home I felt like an unpaid servant but when I was at work it was different. I worked full time Players cigarette manufacturing company factory. There were hundreds of men and women working there and the atmosphere was good. I was a bit of a rogue to some of the older women. I would torment some of them but a lot of the women took a shine to my happy-go-lucky attitude. They said I was a breath of fresh air. I was just 15 when I started work and I kept myself to myself. I told no one my business because I had been brought up that way but some of them knew me Mam had died because Aunt Bess got me the job and she had told them. A couple of women took me under their wing; they looked after me and even invited me to their homes. I have kept in touch with some of the people I used to work with although a lot of the older ladies have since died. It was at work that I felt safe and normal. My personality began to shine through the tough exterior and people liked me for who I was. I enjoyed my job and worked hard. Everyone appreciated my enthusiasm and I was highly thought of. There were always people at work asking me to work with them. I felt valued as an individual and I was treated as an equal.

As soon as I arrived home I could feel myself changing. I became grumpy and my personality changed but this only lasted as long as I was at home. When I got paid Dad took it all off me. He would give me back enough for my bus fare for the following week and that was it. If I wanted anymore I had to ask for it. Often when he was drunk he would say take a pound out of me trousers; I only ever took what he said even though I had access to more.

I just got on with my life because I felt as though I could not change anything. This was my lot for now, the young uns looked up to me and asked me questions about growing up. I never fobbed them off with "You will find out one day." Just as me Mam would say or "You will know soon enough." Or "It's grown up stuff." Or "You will learn that later." I was never given a straight answer to any question I asked so in the end you learn not to ask questions. But the young uns asked questions and I told them the answers, I made sure of that. If they asked a question I did my best to give an honest answer, if I didn't know the answer I would look for the answer in a book.

After I left school, my pain was so far buried I chose to forget it for many years. Dad never touched me again, he treated me as a fairly normal person still a slave to the housework but that I could handle after all that's all I knew from a very early age. He was still controlling and verbally abusive but I coped with that. I felt he was always worried in case I left home so he had to keep me on his side. Would he cope with a job and three kids under the age of eight I wondered? I was growing up; my school years had come to an end. He would ask me questions about my relationships and ask if I had sex with boys, which of course I did not. I never wanted to, I had no interest in sex at all, I was too scared at the very thought of it. I had toughened up a bit but was still very reserved where lads were concerned.

Dad had forced me to leave school and get a job. The school said I might get my CSE's, if I stayed on and I had a good chance of getting through them, with some hard work, even though I had missed a lot of school due to my Mam being ill. My Dad always said women should be at home with the children and look after their men. He was a very chauvinistic man, the truth was that he had no respect for women and he wanted me at work because he wanted the money I could earn. My aunt sorted out a factory job for me and I did enjoy it very much. I made some new friends and began to go out more. I suppose I started to get myself a little independence. I met boys and went out with some but they were all interested in one thing and I wasn't, so again the name calling started. They would say I was frigid and they would ask why I didn't have sex with them. I used to reply because I was a good girl and did not want sex with them. The truth was I was too terrified it was too painful to even think about. They soon got fed up with waiting and dumped me or just did not turn up for the next date.

CHAPTER THIRTY-FOUR

ANOTHER WOMAN

The time flew by after Mam died. I never saw or heard anything to suspect Dad was abusing either of my sisters they did talk to me and ask questions. They came to me for everything and I loved them like I was their Mam. I lost my temper loads of times with them because I still had to do everything in the house. No one helped me with the cleaning or the cooking and I was fed up of feeling like the family slave. When I was their age I was cleaning, cooking and looking after them but they did not have to do anything because I still did all the fetching and carrying not just for them but for my Dad and brothers too. Life went on and I didn't mind really because it was my job and I was used to it. Even though at times I got angry with them I knew it was not their fault. They were still young and they missed out on Mam's love and affection, they were suffering in their own way. We all suffer in our own way, life is hard but hopefully we grow stronger through it all.

Eventually Dad found himself a woman down the pub that he brought home to meet us. She was nice and eventually he started staying at her place for weekends, which in one way was good as it helped him to adjust to his new life without Mam, and yet James became controlling over us all so we did not gain any peace; in fact it was as bad. He would shout at us, order us to do things and hit us. This meant Dad had little or no time for us at all, which suited me just fine. I felt I could not win. I was very unhappy but just left to get on with it. I continued with my chores: cleaning, cooking and taking care of the young uns. I had turned another corner where my Dad was concerned he spoke to me a little more civil he seemed happy which I was happy about. Then Dad and this woman fell out and he met another woman who he stayed with for a number of years again he stayed out at weekends only this time I was growing up and wanted to go out myself but instead I baby sat every weekend the girls from work asked me to go out I said I couldn't so they said stand up to him he is ruining your life (if only they knew) so I did stand up to him and asked if we could compromise and do alternate weekends he flipped his lid but eventually saw my point of view and admitted I was becoming a woman myself, but he waited up for me every time I went out and if a boy brought me home he said something to them when he saw them out of the gate and made sure I never saw them again they stood me up on the next date. I never knew what he said but it always did the trick.

God was not in my life and I rarely prayed, as I did not know how to anymore. God dumped me and as he was not there for me when I most needed him, He was out of my life. I never went to church and only had a handful of friends. I longed for one special friend who I could spill out all my feelings to but that didn't happen, not yet anyway. I just bottled everything up and buried it deep down inside my soul.

When I was 17 I was invited to go down town to a few nightclubs with a friend from work and although we did not drink we did dance. I loved dancing and I danced until the early hours at a club called the Ad Lib. The DJ played mostly Motown and Soul music, some other stuff as well but Motown was my favourite. I met a man who said he really liked me after we had danced for a while. I had seen him before but we did not know each other, only by sight on the dance floor. He was much older than me at around 25, but my mind was made up, it was time I found something out. I needed someone who I did not want to get involved with. Of course I fancied him a little but he was really my guinea pig, so to speak. After the club finished about midnight, he asked me back to his flat for sex and I agreed. After we had sex he telephoned a taxi and I went straight home. I did not even know his name. I felt cheap but I desperately needed to know if I was damaged inside this is something I had to do. I had no feelings for this man neither did he for me. I have to say I expected more from my first time with a guy, it was a nothing

155

experience no more than a quickie and that's what it was. He did me the courtesy of walking me to a taxi and that was that, I never saw him again not even down the club.

I began to wonder if I was a bad person I felt guilty for what I had agreed to. He didn't know he was a means to an end for me, a nothing, non-descript bonk, no other way of saying it really. I never felt anything, no pain, no emotion; my experience just left me hollow. I felt dirty giving myself to a stranger. I did not like it nor did I want it again in a hurry, I felt ashamed at what I had done but at least I knew now that I was not damaged inside. I think I was mentally scarred from my past, so it would never happen again until I met the man I was to marry.

Lads must have thought I was fairly attractive, I was 5.5 in height nice slim build not thin but not fat, I had long brown hair and had a nice disposition always happy and chatty when I was away from home, I had a little of Jackal and Hyde in me I guess. I was never short of male friends and indeed boyfriends I enjoyed male company and the dating went on, each date came to the same abrupt ending as soon as their hands began wandering I was off or I just did not turn up for the next date or they didn't turn up. Either way the break ups were all about what was in a man's trousers, a kiss in a shop doorway or a bus shelter led to a snog which I was happy with then being young that gave the lad a hard on and I froze like a bag of peas, it was time to escape I would say on yer bike, they might be a little forceful because let's face it once a lad has a hard on they seem to lose control. I remember on more than one occasion I slapped their face and ran off, and once the lad was getting verbal and forceful a little too aggressive for me so I jumped on the nearest bus which took me miles away from where I lived and with little money I wondered how I would ever get home but after explaining to the bus driver what had happened he got me on the right bus without paying. I don't know how but I was in my own home in no time at all.

I decided that sex was for the male species for their own gratification and women were a means to an end for them and I was having none of it until I was ready to Love and Trust the lad which was when I was 19, and even then I was with him months before the natural progression happened.

CHAPTER THIRTY-FIVE

DAVID

I met David, I really liked him he was no dancer, but handsome, tall and slim with brown hair. I had a lot of feelings for him he treated me with respect at least for the first week or two then he felt he needed some return for him taking me out, he had a van with a mattress in the back. I just looked at it and said no and if you had any respect for me you will wait. He told me he was falling in love with me and wanted to show me his feelings by having sex, I said no.

Weeks turned into months we were still together going out having a good time and he asked me every single weekend is now the right time, I said no we just kissed I did not want sex I feared sex.

Then after 8 months I took bad with the flu real flu I was ill in bed he knocked on the door and Dad let him in and said she is in bed ill go up and see her, I was horrified he gently kissed me then talked a little then his hands went under my bed sheets and started groping me I asked him to stop but he carried on. I felt so ill but I jumped up and slapped his face, and told him to get out, I said No!

He ran down the stairs without a word and slammed the front door.

Two weeks later we bumped into each other, he asked me were we still a couple. I said no and he cried and said sorry but felt he had waited long enough and if two people loved each other it was natural to want sex and if I had him back he would wait for me so we began dating again but he was like an octopus, I was so scared it would be like the man with no name, we were in his van one night in a country lane and I made up my mind this was the night, I was going to give in. I had prepared myself mentally we began kissing. David was so gentle and caring we were just starting to get intimate when he had a massive nose bleed there was blood gushing from his nose it was all over us, our clothes were covered he tried to stop it, but it only slowed down a little enough time for us to get home, David's Dad gave me a lift home after we said good night.

I got home and cleaned myself up and went to bed. Dad was at his lady friend's so no explaining was necessary. I lay in bed and God spoke to me in no uncertain terms this man is not for you wait a true love will be yours one day, I sat up and thought the nose bleed must be a sign from God. Sex was never meant to happen with David and it never did even though I thought I loved him I finished with him, and my heart turned over every time I saw him. I wanted him so bad but I did not give in I took notice of my instincts, he was 2 years older than me and went on to marry but his marriage only lasted 6 months it was said by his friend he was really still in love with me and that I had come between them as a couple, and that I had broken his heart, I never said but my heart was broken too by our split, I have to say I was flattered but felt sorry for the girl whom I had never met, he had married her on the rebound. We was never going to get back together again it became just another memory.

CHAPTER THIRTY - FIVE

PAUL

Some months later I met Paul down the Palae DE dance in Nottingham we talked until two am when we got thrown out what we talked about was unbelievable, we instantly hit it off, I met with him the following Sunday and again we knew it was right an instant attraction we had a good time, we enjoyed each others company, always had fun even if we were in a group of teenager's Paul was an apprentice and also went to college at night we did not have much money but we laughed, I always caught the same bus home, it was the last bus home from Maid Marian Way he saw to that, in those day the drivers were more understanding and if I was not there on time he would wait for me and shout "Come on, no time for kissing tonight get on the bus or I am going without you." The drivers got to know the regulars in those days, I would say bye and jump on the bus, whilst the driver was smiling and pulling away he shouted "bye see you tomorrow". Paul and I were inseparable so it was time to introduce him to friends and family he was liked but one older friend said he is not right for you Marie he will break your heart, I told her I loved him already I just knew I did, Paul was handsome he had long brown curly hair, no clothes, no car couldn't even drive, and no money but always looked clean was always polite and treated me like I was a queen with dignity, he was caring it was as if he completely understood me without knowing any of my past this was my first real love, we respected each other here and now, no hang ups the kiss led to a snog and he was happy so long as I was happy we always left each other with an ache in our hearts and could not wait until the next date, none of us had telephones at home and mobiles did not exist we made arrangements and waited sometimes a week in between, that was true Love.

I have always been in love with him and he was willing to wait until I was completely ready for sex, no not sex, an embrace for love in the sheets because he loved me too. We met when I was nearly nineteen and Dad was absolutely horrible to him. He would make him stay at the garden gate in all weathers until I had finished all my jobs and if there was no one to look after the young uns I had to stay home. It was hard at times but we really loved each other and that was stronger than the hate I had for my Dad, so we coped with whatever was thrown at us, and things began to settle down it was a test of true love because any other boy would have run a mile with a Dad like mine, but I learnt much later that Paul had a past too and he too, he also had a Dad who was often violent and had a penniless up bringing maybe that's why we jelled we had things in common, so for all our miserable pasts God brought two people together to have joy and laughter for the rest of our lives.

Time passed on it was now 1973. Paul and I began to plan our future together we had an engagement party at the Heart of the Midlands. There were artists performing on stage at the club. I wore a powder blue maxi dress edged in fluffy fur and Paul wore a burgundy shirt and black trousers. It was an open invitation so anyone could come as long as they paid for themselves. About 25 people arrived at our party and we had a very nice evening. My engagement ring was shaped like a little heart, there was a Blue Sapphire surrounded by three tiny diamonds. It was not very expensive £22.50 but it was special; I loved my engagement ring and loved the person who gave it to me.

I told Dad I would now pay him £5.00 per week for my board, instead of giving him my whole wage packet, as I needed to save for the wedding. Dad hit the roof "What wedding you are not getting married he will never marry you, and who will help me? Don't you care about the young uns anymore? And you better not be having sex I will have words with him" "I am not listening Dad anybody would think I meant tomorrow, I will not let you burst my bubble a wedding is in our plans so get used to the idea." I only earned £12.00 a week. Dad did not argue about the money but handed me one of the bad debts he had accumulated and told me I had to pay it off here this is yours he said. It was from a shop called Kristi's; everything in this shop was bought on credit. It sold clothes, household things and furniture. Dad bought all our clothes from this shop but he didn't pay off the debt. Then to make things worse he bought some clothes for his lady friend, that cost around £87, and he handed the bill to me and said, "You will have to pay this." I just yelled at him but it was no good, he said, "Growing up comes with responsibilities look it's in your name I have paid some off for you." I had to pay it off before I could start saving for my wedding. I don't know how he did it but the account was in my name.

I worked more and more overtime to pay off the debts. I needed as much extra money as I could get my hands on, the debts were eventually paid it took about a year of hard labour by myself, as soon as I paid it off I went into the shop and closed the account, I also told the women my Dad opened it in my name and not to let this happen again.

Paul and I saved as much as we could and eventually we started to plan our wedding for September 1974. It was a simple inexpensive but beautiful wedding. I wore a beautiful wedding gown, which was a copy of a French designed bridal gown. I had a picture of the dress I wanted cut out from a catalogue and Dad knew a dressmaker down the Red Lion who charged very little to copy the dress. My dress was made from white crimplene fabric. Looking back it was thick and cumbersome but on the day it looked wonderful with a sweet heart neckline and small cap sleeves. It had a small train edged in delicate pink roses. I did not want a veil so I had a white hat and I sewed pink roses onto the back of the hat so it matched the train on my dress. I held a white frilly parasol with fresh roses draping from it and on my hands I wore long silk gloves, which came up to my elbows. I looked and felt very special. Paul and his best man wore grey suits.

We had 3 bridesmaids: June, Carol and Rosanna. To save money I made the three bridesmaid outfits. The fabric was pale pink printed with white roses and I made them in the hope that they would be able to wear them after my big day. The design was a basic pinafore dress and underneath they wore a white frilly blouse and a crocheted Juliet cap that I was able to make because Mam had taught me how to crochet. The bridesmaids also wore little white gloves and each of them carried a Posey arrangement made up of pink and white roses.

We had our wedding reception at my aunt's pub; we did not have to pay for this, as it was her wedding gift to us. It was amazing really to think we had everything we wanted for our wedding on such a tiny budget but this was one day in the rest of our lives together, this was our day.

For our honeymoon we travelled by train to South sea in Portsmouth and we stayed in a small bed and breakfast boarding house, which was very basic, but the people were lovely. I remember it rained every single day but we were happy. We did not have a care in the world as we walked hand in hand along a beach in the rain but I always had a fear in the back of my mind that my happiness could not possibly last.

We took advice from an older friend and we managed to get a 100% mortgage for £4,250.00 to buy our first home. It was a pre war built semi detached house that was scruffy, old, and some of it falling apart but it was ours we stayed at Dad's whilst making it fit to move into, there was no central heating, a pot sink in the kitchen and that was it, it had no cupboards in the kitchen, we managed with coal fires for a long time and travelled from work every night on the bus as we did not have a car yet. We had to strip every wall and planed what we should do to each room, one night it was dark and with no electricity set up yet we were stripping a wall with the light of an industrial torch which Paul got off a building site, I was so tired and it was so cold I sat on the bare boards and fell fast asleep in the wall paper, Paul covered me up with a dust sheet and carried on working until it was time for the last bus, on another occasion again with only the torch for light instead of stripping the walls we stripped each other and just as we finished our christening of our first home together a knock came at the door two policemen stood there, "What's going on here then one policeman said. We explained we were doing the house up striping walls and we had no electricity supply yet, they smiled at one another and said we could see a flash light and some shadows behind your make do curtains, someone reported to us the house may have burglars, they were happy with our explanation and went we laughed and laughed until our ribs ached.

We spent hours upon hours modernising the house, but could not afford furniture. It took every penny we earned but it was ours and we were content that was until Paul was sent away to work in London.

After a few months of making the house habitable Paul and I moved into our new home, which was about 15 miles from my family. It was very painful for me. My family were fending for themselves and Dad met a woman who started to take care of his needs but it meant my brothers and sisters were on their own for long periods of time they were much older now but I was very worried for them and I knew I would miss them.

In our new home we didn't have much, we had nothing other than a sofa which we had been given, we had basic essentials not very much but we were happy and in love. We could not afford any luxuries on our wages as we now had a mortgage and needed every penny to carry on with the modernisation of our home, so my husband and I both went to work every hour we could, far too many hours really. I found it difficult to stop cooking loads of food I cooked enough for 7 people for so many years it was hard to stop, it was hard being without my family and I was struggling to cope, Paul and I hardly saw each other he would work all day and go on day release to college and get home for 10 o'clock in the evening when he would eat his meal. I worked shifts one week 6 till 2.30 or 2 till 9 unless I did double shifts on occasion, we were knackered but still in love and longed to be in each other's arms in our freezing cold house we were still very happy.

When we were just 6 months, Paul had to go to work in London, I was completely alone in our house, which still had missing floorboards upstairs; no heating other than the coal fires the house was an absolute mess. Because we were modernising our home ourselves and happy with each others company we had no problems but when

Paul was taken out of the equation by working away from home, nothing was being done. I was devastated and I fell into a deep depressed state, which I had no control over, I was still cooking for 7 people what was wrong with me? I went to the doctors and they turned me away and said come back next week, so I went home, went to work, went to bed and had nothing in between. I was losing the plot having to get up for work at 05:30 without having had a good night's sleep, getting home at 15:00 completely exhausted one week and leaving my home at 13:00 getting home at 22:00 the second week. I began to feel very ill. I could make no sense of my behaviour. I cooked for 7 people in the morning before I went to work and then when I got home I felt exhausted and thought I was going mad. I decided to go back to the doctor and the receptionist said to come next week again but this time I broke down sinking to the floor in floods of tears. I cried and cried no one could get a word of any sense out of me. I just wept buckets. The receptionist fetched the doctor who was an Asian lady. The doctor shouted at the receptionist saying you never turn away people like this. I was having a breakdown, all my emotions were coming out at once and my body went limp I had no idea how to get up from the floor or how they got me up and took me to a room where I laid down on a bed, and I told her about my Mam dying, about moving away from my sisters and brothers, about my husband going away to work. Everything came tumbling out but not my secret, which was well buried. She said I was having an emotional breakdown and that all my tears, which I had been told to hold back for years and years just kept on coming. The doctor told me all these saved up emotions have to come out eventually, sometimes years after just in your case. She said there are no timescales for inner emotions they will come out when they are ready and that it was now was my time. The doctor prescribed a 3-month course of anti depressant drugs for me. Paul came home for two weeks but had to go back I stood at the gate sobbing. Some weeks pasted and we had a wonderful Christmas together in Spain in the sunshine, we talked and tried to make sense of it. This helped with my recovery and I was finally able to come to terms of what was happening to me. Paul was so supportive, I eventually came off the drugs and went back to work and Paul came home every weekend until his job had come to an end. We bought a telephone and he called me every single night. We were so happy and I was content and very slowly my life started to get back to normal.

In the years to come I grew stronger, unless Dad was around me, then I became weak again. He came to our house for Christmas year after years we moved house nearer to the family, we would see them more often, but Dad also visited us more often. He normally behaved himself at Christmas, a little uncouth but acceptable because Paul was there. He knew he would be taken straight back home alone but one Christmas someone bought him a bottle of whisky, which he decided to polish off at breakfast time. We picked him up later on Christmas Day and when the time came to eat dinner he sat at the table and his head fell right into his dinner. Paul was disgusted. He put him into the car and took him home. The following year we asked the rest of the family to share Christmas with him, we'd had enough, not many of them were willing and he refused to go to anyone else. He just kept saying Marie would fetch me. I said no, so he stayed home alone, as we insisted we had one Christmas on our own. He had me on the run fetching and carrying at his beck and call, why I did it, I have no idea, and he seemed to be in total control of me even though I was now married. He stayed home and he continued to drink heavily, nearly a full bottle of whisky but I still took him a dinner on my way home from church, which remained there on Boxing Day. He was still pulling my strings. One kind of abuse stopped but another had started. I never told Paul the half of what was said because *I did not have an answer as to why I just could not abandon him.* Dad was so nice in front of him and in front of my brothers, so they might have thought I was being paranoid about the way he was, but on this occasion Paul heard the 15 messages he left on our answer phone. This was not a one off either, he used to leave 15-20 messages every day but Paul said, "That's enough. Next year we are not having him and you are not going to take him dinner someone else can." I arranged for him to go to my brothers, but he still telephoned and said "Marie is fetching me so don't fetch me, I don't want to go anywhere else." Only I did not know my arrangements had been cancelled, so he stayed home alone again and drank himself to near death. The next year he ended up in hospital, which ruined our Christmas anyway, he was so selfish.

Paul and I were very happy. We went on holiday every year and sometimes we took my sisters with us. Dad was more independent and he was seeing a woman so that took some of his attention away from us and his demands got fewer but they were always arguing and falling out. Dad's demands were on her now but she was having none of it. It didn't last long and in the end she finished with him and then he would start on us again but our love was strong it did not matter what bullets were fired we could fight them.

Our second home, was much bigger than our first. It had a bigger garden and a small drive, which we needed because we now had a little purple Mini. We were still very happy, money was plentiful and we took frequent holidays. We went out a lot with friends but these nights out were becoming more and more frequent we were drinking not to get drunk purely social drinking but regular.

I had a nagging feeling inside and voices in my head saying I was too happy and it could not last people were not meant to be this happy we loved each other too much, but our happiness continued. When friends asked if we argued, I would say no we never argued yes we had our own opinions but never actually fell out where we did not talk for hours like some of our friends did, we always looked forward to coming home even though we lived in a house that resembled a building site as that's the way we climbed the housing market buying old do uppers as Paul would say

I started to feel that I wanted more and I guess I began to feel a little broody. I always wanted children but Paul and I had never talked about having a family. One evening I decided to raise the subject and I was surprised to discover that Paul felt exactly the same way. It was at this point we decided we would try for our first baby we were both 28 years old.

Getting pregnant was proving to be a difficult task and it was taking much longer than any of us anticipated. My over active imagination started to go into overdrive and I started thinking about my past which I hadn't done for many years. I worried myself to the point that I began to feel ill; *what if my insides had been damaged as a result of what happened to me during my childhood. Oh my God it would all come out to Paul, he would be sure to divorce me. Although I knew he loved me, my fears came back to haunt me, my insecurity of being happy, I did not deserve to be this happy. I kept my secret for so long, the doctors would probably force it out of me and that would be that. Why could I not accept my life was not cursed?*

I eventually fell pregnant but it was not meant to be as I miscarried at 9 weeks. A few months after my first loss, I got pregnant again and this time I only carried for 10 weeks before I miscarried. After the second miscarriage the doctors advised us to wait at least 6 months before trying again to allow my body time to heal but I was worried that my body clock was ticking away.

Eventually I got pregnant again and although it did not get off to a good start the pregnancy slowly settled down. I left the job I loved to become a full time mother and because I was so liked all the gifts we received we did not have to buy anything for our new baby for the first year. The gifts from my work friends covered many tables and consisted of baby clothes in every size, style and colour imaginable. There was a pram, cot, highchair, bath, door swing and nappies in fact if you think what a baby might need in its first year we had it all. When I took home my gifts my family could not believe how popular I was, I could not believe it either. Our lives were now complete. I gave birth to a son in January 1984 and still right at the back of my mind I had constant niggles that someone would take away Paul or our son away. I just could not shake it off, why couldn't I enjoy my happiness after all I was free of my dad's demands, at least for now my own mind felt guilty for feeling happy.

We thanked God together when our son was born and asked God to always protect him. My life was suddenly turned upside down and God was back in my life. He came back with the birth of our son and I began to pray again for the first time in many years. In my prayers I thanked God for my happiness but still in my head I had a tormented day dream which told me my elation could not last. My Dad started phoning me every 10 minutes for stupid things he wanted he was starting to take away my joy; he was slowly beginning to take over my life again. I think it was because we lived fairly close to him and he was on my doorstep when I came home from shopping. I wanted him to be part of our life but he was in my vision most of the time.

When our son was a year old I went back to work for a few hours each week. Paul walked in from work and I walked out to work like ships passing in the night. I only did 3 hours a night and it was good for all of us.

My church life grew stronger and I now ran the toddler group during the day. Paul and I decided we wanted to try for another baby but it was never meant to be. I suffered a further 2 miscarriages early on in the pregnancies and then I had an ectopic pregnancy. At 12 weeks I lost twins with one in the tube and one in the womb neither of them could be saved in total we lost 6 babies.

Paul and I were devastated by yet another loss, it was horrible and we felt it was all too much. Within 2 weeks the doctor dropped yet another bombshell on us; he strongly advised me to have a hysterectomy because I had nearly lost my life during my last pregnancy and it had damaged my insides. He went on to say that I could have the operation within a month. I was sent to another room to give it some thought but a decision had to be made that day. *How could I make this decision alone? I needed Paul to help me; we made all our decisions this together.*

I was crying when a nurse came in and she said, "Look, this is your body, it is really your decision at the end of the day. You cannot afford to get pregnant again or your little boy will not have a mother. Ring your husband." I stared at her and said "How can I tell him something like this over the phone?" I eventually agreed to have the operation but in my mind I knew I could always change my mind after I'd discussed it with Paul.

In the end Paul and I decided that I should have the operation, which was arranged in 2 months time. Paul was very upset but acknowledged the decision had to be made for the good of my health and son. We were blessed with one healthy boy and we are grateful for him.

When our son was 5 and at school I got a new job managing a

Christian Coffee Shop, which was run by a board of trustees and was a charitable trust. I had 30 volunteers on the books and I would cook, supervise and chat with the customers often about God. My faith had grown immensely and now I was helping others to find their way to God's door. My local vicar told me that my skills as an evangelist were good and that I should always keep up the good work. I read the bible every day and improved my knowledge on the word of God. I was not fanatical or a 'God basher'. I was happy in my job and if I could help people in my walk with God then that was better than keeping it to myself.

I had found God and wanted others to know about him too.

Ann was a person who went to the same church as me and we thought it was a good idea for her to occupy one of the rooms above the café to do Christian counselling for anyone who wanted it, which included the staff I worked with. Ann sat in a room once a week, and nearly always had someone with problems to chat to.

CHAPTER THIRTY-SIX

STABILITY

I have heard many times of people going off the rails after abuse, turning to sex, drugs, alcohol, depression, self-harm, religion, bulimia and anorexia. I have to say I believe I had the start of bulimia in my early teenage years, being sick after eating but I think deep down I realised before it got out of hand, perhaps Mam was watching over me. I have heard of people even carrying the pattern of abuse on to their offspring. I did not turn to any of those things; I guess I was lucky.

Yes, I had a faith but I quietly believed in God, I prayed from my heart, in silence. Although I left God for a good number of years after Mam died, my faith never left me and I eventually went back to Him. I had not been to church for along time as Dad would not allow me to and as a teenager my Christian belief was there but I never practised although looking back I wish I had I feel I missed out on my faith although as I went through my years of torment I gained an inner strength from somewhere and that stayed with me. Oh I had some major relapses during my adult life but I was never defeated and I now know I never will be.

The jobs I had throughout my working life have always been a challenge. I have never been able to settle in one job for too long. I always wanted more, so I studied hard and always got the job applied for. I will never be rich as none of my jobs were highly paid executive jobs but I always managed to hold down a job and people liked me for my personality. Finally, I was starting to leave all my anger behind. I have a happy disposition always have had but I am very hard on myself. At times I challenge myself with jobs, which are perhaps a little too difficult for me to cope with, but I always give it my best shot and eventually reach my goal. Even though the challenge sometimes gets me down and makes me cry and feel frustrated that I could have done better with my schooling and career, I get on with the job I have learnt. Then I am not satisfied with it anymore because it's no longer a challenge and I have to move on, but that's me and that's maybe a fault of mine or my uneasy past, I am not sure.

As my Dad got older he got nastier and more hateful toward me. I coped until my healing began at the age of 34. Then I found I could not go to see him for a while and I did not go to the house for around three months.

Dad called me names because I went to church regularly and he cursed God for guiding me. My Dad was jealous of God, he actually said that and he tried to stop me going by saying it's not real. He would blaspheme about God and religion and would say I was not worthy to go to church after the past I'd had. He was really worried about my going to church and I never quite realised why until much later. I had blocked my secrets out, but he was living in fear they would emerge and he would be found out I am sure of that.

Whatever I did for Dad was wrong he ridiculed my actions constantly. If I shopped for him the shopping was not right, he would even write a list but it was still wrong if I cooked it was wrong, if I ironed his clothes they were wrong. He just kept battering me down, and was still very much in controlling me.

I remember I took him to his sisters for the weekend and he treated me like a servant. I washed his socks and hung them out to dry. He went crazy and said I had not hung them on the line the right way up. He said they were upside down and he called me useless. My uncle was not impressed and hugged me and said, "He never changes does he?" "He has always been a bombastic nasty man." I just went to my room and kept out of his way. He just made me feel useless with every word he spoke to me and I would pray that one day I would just be able to get one thing right for him, so he would be proud of me.

After that I cut down on the visits as I still worked and had my own family. I went to see him once a week and cleaned for him. Each time I sat outside his house, I trembled with the hatred I felt for him and yet I was compelled to look after him. I would pray before I got out of the car, the vicars wife told me to put Gods armour on before I went into the house, so I did and it helped me to cope with the next verbal abuse.

Jesus, my heavenly father, give me the courage and strength, to go in that house, and then I would put on God's armour, my shield, my sandals, my helmet, just as it says in the Bible. It made me feel able to cope and could do what I considered to be my duty. Even though I only went once a week he still rang me 15 times a day but I ignored most of the calls, as he wanted me to go to his house. He said he needed supplies of food when he did not. It was mainly so he could shout abuse at me but he was a very lonely man with no friends and no family who cared for him. He had 4 sons and 3 daughters who did not like him because he was arrogant and ignorant. Most of them visited him once or twice a year with the exception of my sisters who visited on a regular basis who loved him as a Dad should be loved. He returned this love to them; he was mostly nice to them, but not always.

I learnt to live with his foul and abusive language. If he swore or shouted at me I said nothing, not even a goodbye. I just walked out and shut the door and went home. I was not standing for it anymore I was learning after all these years I was leaning to shut him out. He would then ring and ring until I went again. When he took ill, I was at the hospital on one occasion when he punched a nurse whilst she was making his bed. He was still as strong as an ox even when he was ill. They called for security; he asked for a drink and threw it over the uniformed man and said "Leave me alone and began quoting some words from Hitler. It took four men to hold him down whilst they injected him to calm him down. I just stood watching in disbelief. I was ashamed to call him my Dad. The hospital staff were lovely and said he had senile dementia. I told them he had always been a nasty cantankerous man. At the very end when he was dying, The nurse told me he shouted down the ward Marie I want Marie she is the only person who understands me, but I was not there for him, I arrived 10 minutes after his death.

Around his deathbed I never cried, my tears had flowed throughout my life and now there were none. In fact I felt released, a sense of peace flowed through me. I suddenly felt relaxed, I was free, free from torture, verbal abuse, pain, slavery, criticism, fear, my incapability to do things right, everything that my Dad stood for suddenly left me. I felt a strange kind of well being, released from the strong hold he had over me. My tension began to slowly ease, my nightmares stopped and my tears were past.

Then I felt guilty for feeling relieved he was dead. Can you believe that? It felt as though he was punishing me from the grave.

I then began to find myself, believe in myself, I found self worth, my confidence started to return, and my own true happiness. I had more time, I was free of a burden yes he was my burden, which had been on my shoulders for all my years, and my memories will always be there. We can never erase the memories from our minds, but God has filled the void in my heart, which my Dad once filled. Dad was once in control of my thoughts, of my very existence. He caused my sadness and all of my so-called childhood had been snatched away. I would never get those years back, I am a woman now and the loss of my Dad was a freedom no one else in the family could ever understand with the exception of James maybe?

The memories are now beginning to fade a little. The pain has been released slowly, now I have forgiven Dad, Mam and my brother.

So I can now get on with the rest of my life in peace and harmony with God as my friend. I often wonder how I would be if my life had been different but I suppose my personality comes from my life as it was. I have empathy with people in pain, and sympathy for people who have been in my position. Mostly, I absolutely love my life now, and have put my past in the past; it's now buried with my Dad. You cannot change what happened yesterday, but you can look forward to tomorrow. I am happy, I am content with my life; it is good, really good. I have survived the horrors of my childhood.

CHAPTER THIRTY- SEVEN

JUNE

June was the only person I told whilst Dad was alive. I asked her to come over to stay for the night and we talked over a bottle of wine. She hardly ever went to see Dad after we'd talked. She hated him for what he had done which is why I decided never to tell the others until after his death. I did not want hatred to run through the family. June was full of compassion towards me and she felt my pain but her hatred for Dad ran deep and still does today, which I feel guilty about. June promised that she would not tell another soul and she understood when I told her it was my decision to make regarding, who and when I told. Although she reluctantly agreed not to tell anyone I could not stop the hatred she started to feel against Dad.

June wanted me to go to the Police to report the abuse I had suffered at the hands of our Dad but I couldn't. He was at that point a pathetic, frail old man so what purpose would reporting him to the Police serve. His family despised him without knowing my secret. He suffered without prison because of his loneliness, his own thoughts of the wickedness and pain he had caused others and later he suffered with crippling lung disease, which eventually took his life. No, it was my final decision not to take it any further. I had no real answers as to why this or why that because I did not know the answers myself. I feel I handled the situation the best way I could. It needed to be spoken about. I did not choose my time easily; I truly believe it was in God's time and just pray it was right both for my family whom I love dearly and myself who could cope with the upheaval of my life.

I was seeing the light after the nightmare that was in my deepest memory for so long.

I was at last feeling free from the guilt of the dark secret, which held me back from living a full life.

A TV programme hosted by Esther Rantzen helped to bring my worst nightmare to the surface. She said, "Children and adults alike need to talk about the past." I did and it burst the bubble right in my face and I had to deal with it. Luckily with God's help and in his time, and also with the help of a Christian counsellor who gave no advice, who did not judge me, who just listened and believed me. That was the most important thing, she believed me, after all who could imagine such a story. We prayed God would fill the empty hole, which my pain had filled for so long. The 8 sessions and many years to follow (which was no time at all considering I had carried it for more than 28 years) brought healing. I felt at peace for two years. Then bang, another balloon popped in my face, another surfacing of pain rose up from the inner being, which was not expected, after all I thought I had been healed.

CHAPTER THIRTY-EIGHT

THE PARCEL

I believe God was with me from the day on the beach and maybe even before that. He watched my family and I suffer. I do not understand why we had to go through the pain we did. I thrashed it out in my mind but came up with nothing no answers to any of my questions. The only thing I came up with was in the bible and it said Man has been given free will. I do not question it anymore because although I will never forget my past, I did learn to forgive my Dad with God's help. Circumstances are a major part in each person's life and it's up to us to deal with each circumstance as it arises; you can let it take over your life or let it go. Some people have worse nightmares than I had, and I pray to God they can come to terms with them.

I have now laid my past in a brown parcel tied up with string at the foot of the cross, and it is still there, I check periodically, and I see it there on the step, I do not want it back even though it's a large chunk of my life, and giving it to God left a gaping hole in my heart which I filled with God's unconditional Love for me, all my childhood was taken away through circumstance, I have given my past to God. I still feel pain every now and then and still shed tears and I feel sorry for myself on occasion and wonder what it would have been like if things were different, but my life is healing as time goes on and no amount of what ifs can change what happened.

I hope one day all who have suffered in a similar way to me can also experience my kind of healing.

CHAPTER THIRTY-NINE

OWN AGENDA

I was asked by a member of the church to go on a retreat to a convent just to have some personal time with God. I knew her quite well and she offered to drive as she wanted to go too but not on her own and Paul did not mind having a weekend on his own. I really needed some 'me' time. There were seminars and quiet times to reflect, singing and people giving testimonies of times in their life, which they had been healed from. A man was talking as if to me, and was saying that I had not brought everything to God for forgiveness and I just fell apart for no apparent reason. I wept buckets of tears and did not know why. I left the hall. My friend was not sitting near me so I went into a quiet prayer room where I sat alone, with a flickering candle. It was amazing, the silence began to calm me, then two nuns entered the room, and prayed for me with no questions. They did not ask why I was upset and to be honest I did not know why myself so they prayed not knowing what for. They just prayed into the silence. They sat opposite me with their hands on their laps facing upwards and I sat with my hands in a similar way. I began crying uncontrollably and in the prayer the most amazing thing happened. I felt someone holding my hand it was warm and gentle soft and caring. When I looked the two nuns had not moved they were in the same position. They said in prayer to put my pain into a parcel, tie it up and lay it at the foot of the cross. My innermost fears came tumbling out. I told them I had been healed of my past but I felt guilty for telling my brothers and sisters, and how I knew they were hurting and feeling my pain after I told them. The nuns prayed for the guilt to be released, my guilt of telling the family who listened and then buried my secret deep inside themselves ashamed because they were not able to help me. I was so troubled by the fact I had to tell them. The nuns said my guilt would go away today and it did. I now pray for my brothers and sisters healing and release because it may sound strange, they now carry my wounded heart. Sometimes I wish I had never told them but it had to be said. I needed to know if it was just me or were others involved. James and I are as close as we used to be, I believe we have a special bond. My bruises have healed, but he still lives with his bruises, as he has no faith to heal him. Maybe one day God will heal him too.

I look to the cross in my mind almost daily to check if that parcel is still there and Thank God it is I do not want it back.

Over the years of my healing process I have spoken to several different women, who just opened up to me without my knowledge of them being abused or them of me, and each story is so different, I am not a counsellor on paper but I know I have counselled lots of people on my travels just by listening and believing their story.

The brief true stories that follow are real, I believe I was lucky, Sensible, God was with me, whatever it was I came to terms with my Demons and was healed both of fear and abuse.

Sammy who is now 35, left home at 16 after she told her family. Her entire family abandoned her because they did not believe her. She has no faith and is full of hatred, which is welling up inside her like a volcano about to erupt. She has her own children now and that is her world. She could not stay in a relationship and said she will never forgive any of her family and totally ignores them if she sees them.

Susan is about 43 years old, she, like me had a faith in God and has come to forgive her abuser, which was her husband, she is still with him. He was on drugs. At the time she claimed he needed help and he did not know what he was doing. He is now off drugs and they are happy, and the families have become closer for the forgiveness and all believe in God as a result.

Elisa now 35 could not live with the pain of her past and went on to self-harm. Elisa is on lots of drugs for depression and she has attempted suicide several times. She will only be healed with God's help, her abuser was her father and his friends. She has been in and out of mental hospitals since her teens, I still pray for her even though I never see her.

Their own brother abused Angelina, who is now 53, along with her sister. Their Mam never believed them, so she is full of hatred for some of her family. None of them believed her story, they said she was just a troublemaker and they have nothing to do with her now. She is so filled with anger and hatred toward everyone she meets that she drinks alcohol to numb her pain. She argues with everyone she meets and said she hates anything to do with religion because if there were a God why would these things happen to innocent children. I did not have an answer to her question, I only know it happened to me also and I felt the same way for a while.

Marge aged 42 was abused by her father and never forgave him but he died whilst she was in her 20s, so she just shut it all out. Although she opened up to me, she never wants to discuss it with anyone she said she was ashamed of her life, she has no faith but she has managed to get on with her life again, with alcohol as her friend.

Anne, after her abuse, had a massive weight problem because food was her comfort as with many oversized people, she became bulimic and was very ill. I heard she eventually died from her illness because she refused to get treatment. She just wanted out because she just could not live with the pain her uncle had caused her during the sexual abuse.

I was once asked if I would change my past. What a question. I do not know the answer, as I have no control over my past, it's done, it's gone by. We can only look forwards to a better future. We cannot wipe the slate clean or take out our memories and wash them pure. We now have to learn to live with our experiences in the hope it has taught us to forgive and be better people as a result of our tormented past. The answer: I loved my Mam and my Dad and I do not know what went wrong with Dad's mixed up evil intentions and as he saw no wrong in his behaviour until the day he died, he did suffer he died a very angry un-liked man, the clock cannot be turned back. I believe he went to his grave without any sort of confession or remorse so therefore he is not with God and he will pay the price for his wrong doings.

I was asked how could you have possibly have forgiven your Dad? Some of the people did not forgive and where did it get them. I believe in God and he forgives all, so why shouldn't I forgive? God does not forgive those who have no forgiveness in their hearts and I wanted to be part of God's plan. I have a place in Heaven and I don't think I am a religious nut. I just have a strong but gentle faith in God.

I had many years living with a painful heart; years when I rebelled against teachers, work colleagues and even myself. I hated myself for what happened in my past, I blamed myself not my Dad. It was me who felt dirty; it was me who went to him. I let the atrocities happen, but I hated myself even more for not being able to forgive my Dad years before I actually did. I only forgave in God's strength, not my own. Once I had forgiven him I felt released, I felt free of my prison cell, which I had been in for so many years. God helped me over the obstacles, which held me back from living a truthful and peaceful life. Life can be cloudy with only evil thoughts and a power so strong it eats away at you, it destroys your inner being and so we all need forgiveness.

I am now healed from my sin and my Dad knows I have forgiven him even though he was dead when my true healing began. He knows he is forgiven and my Mam has been forgiven also, in some ways she was as bad as him as she knew what was happening. Part of my healing was me being able to say I forgive, not because I condone their actions, because I don't, they were wrong. I did nothing wrong and if it has happened to you, you have done nothing wrong either.

I have complete empathy for people who share their deepest secrets with me. I have never sympathised, as this does not help. They need ears, which believe without criticism or accusation, and a friend to be there for them.

I never wanted sympathy. I wanted someone to believe my story to just believe that what I was saying was the truth. These are not fantasising stories. These are atrocities that really happened. The disbelief from some people is the reason for so many men and women holding onto their secrets and pain until they die some people never live a full life because of the heartache they carry.

EPILOGUE

I carried my secret until I was thirty-four. Then it all came tumbling out, both to my sister June first then my husband whilst Dad was alive, and after Dad died to the rest of the family. The response I got from my family was mixed. My two eldest brothers said why did I let it happen, why didn't I tell them? They said they would have sorted him out, and one brother asked how could I go to see him as an adult and why did I look after him in later years? How could I have possibly have had him in my home when my son was born, Dad was a paedophile. They said they could have protected me as a child. All these questions were asked but how could they help me, when they were not there.

Everyone can say I could have helped but we will never know. They did not see the bigger picture, they could not possibly understand or know the daily, emotional blackmail I had from Dad. I loved my family and was frightened, no terrified that we would all be split into different homes and we would have been, because the five youngest were all under 16. We would have ended up in a children's home, just like Dad said. If they had sorted him out, how would they have done it? They could have punched the living daylight out of him, but would that have helped? It certainly would not have changed what had already happened, and might have made matters worse. They could have killed him and then they would have ruined their own lives. I was a child and I had to live there alongside him praying he would not touch the others.

My brother James was disgusted and repulsed by the whole thing it made him physically ill for a while. He was feeling my pain along with his own, because we were both abused in different ways. I think

I caused him more pain for which I am sorry. Robert reacted pretty much in the same way as Carol did. They were intrigued by my story and wanted to know details because they were so young it was hard for them to understand. I could never reveal to them the whole story. They loved their Dad, what right had I to spoil that. They were sad that the perpetrator was their Dad and maybe some of the family did make their own judgment but none of them have ever discussed their feelings with me maybe they couldn't, maybe they have now buried their story, maybe they too get upset and would rather think it never really happened. All these maybes, none of them really matter anymore, it was a long time ago so get over it one member of the family said.

Whilst it was not easy I did get over it but the memories still remain.

ACKNOWLEDGEMENTS

I would like to thank each member of my family, whom I love dearly, for not turning away from me when I told them about what happened behind closed doors. I especially thank June who was my confidante, who never questioned or judged me, but was a pair of ears when I was feeling down, a hug when I was in tears and who had a simple word of encouragement when I needed it.

Thanks especially to my husband Paul who helped me through each part of the healing process, simply by just being there by my side. He was not a judge or jury he was my ever-loving husband, there to give me a hug, with no words to say. Sometimes words were not appropriate when my emotions were in tatters because unless you have experienced what I went through it's hard to find the correct words to say. Not knowing what was around the next corner, each day was another day of healing and sun begun to shine and I was becoming a whole person, the real Marie.

I would also like to thank my Christian counsellor who believed my unravelling deep secret, and who encouraged some of my innermost memories to surface. They were extremely painful, the tears kept falling until my eyes were burnt and bloodshot, until I did not know what to do or think next. My inner-most feelings had to surface with the ugliness of my memories which had to be coaxed out of my heart and mind and which my soul wanted to hang on to, for fear of what may happen next. With gentle probing and hours of prayer, and tears enough to fill 10 buckets Anne sat with me. At times I would say, "No I've had enough" as the memories were far too painful. It would have been easier to just bury them back deep into my soul for ever but my life would have been so different without this healing process. Snippets of horror would keep on coming to life but we battled on. I am healed.

REVIEWS

This book draws the reader into the life of a young girl from a working class background, who takes the role of Mum to her younger siblings. Whilst her mother battles with cancer and her father sexually abuses her.

It is a story of survival and love; the change in Marie growing up through the years of puberty into adulthood is remarkable.

Her strong faith in God as a child, which no one could take away, grew ever stronger in her adult years and developed in spite of questions like "Where are you now God?" In contrast most abuse victims become what I would describe in my role as a GP as 'survivors'. How much this is due to the personality of Marie or the work of God in her life no one will know.

Marie now describes herself as healed, her past is a memory along the journey of life, and has no place in her future.

Dr M. Jones

*****

This story was very interesting to read, though owing to the subject matter sometimes quite emotional. It is very difficult subjects, which were dealt with in a way that will, I am sure, offer comfort and insight to others who suffer through the hands of abusers.

This is not, in anyway, a "depressing" read in fact it offers the reader a snapshot of life that whilst relatively recent seems like a bygone age.

The author's love of her family shines through, as does their love for her.

There are many humorous elements, which enable the reader to both laugh and cry.

The story helps the reader to understand that we should be careful when we judge people. We rarely know the complete story and can often be wrong.

The role of the author's struggle with, and eventual strength gathered from, her faith underpins the book.

This was obviously a very difficult project for the author to undertake but it has been completed wonderfully. You must be very proud that a story for so long hidden is revealed in such a caring and compassionate way.

I have, and still do offer my services as an individual counselor to victims of various traumas. In this capacity I feel the author has made remarkable strides in accepting and dealing with the events in her early life. Obviously she takes great comfort from her faith and the support in later life of her husband and church. I feel sure that the empathy she feels and transmits to others will be of great comfort.

S. Padley

*****

When I first read this story I was overcome with both happy and sad emotions. My initial thought was that I wanted to go out and buy a dolls house for this young girl.

This is a compelling book, which was difficult to put down. As you read about the deep trauma this young girl suffered as a result of her own father abusing her and the verbal abuse which continued into her adult life you realise that her faith in God was justified in the end although it did not seem that way to her during the teenage years of her life.

It is a very moving story with humour, grief and sadness and well worth reading over and over again.

Anonymous

*****

I have known Marie for approximately 25 years she is the most wonderful person you could wish to meet. I often heard her talk of her family, the love she holds for them is immeasurable.

Thinking back to our conversations Marie was sometimes on the brink of admission to this past life she kept buried inside her soul. We often talked about other children who were abused and we prayed for them. I sometimes wondered how deep it was with Marie as she would get so upset it must have rekindled her own painful memories; a secret she held tight when she heard of others suffering in this way.

Her secret was well kept as she states in the book. I believe it was right for her to release all her pain and memories at an age when she could cope with this traumatic event. In her own mind telling anyone at the time would have caused not only more pain for herself but pain for her brothers and sisters who may have been split up as a result of the situation.

Marie was and is today a selfless beautiful person who underwent a totally unnecessary evil at her father's hand and with God's help she was released.

Being a vicar, I often hear people say why does God allow these awful things to happen. I do not have the answers, I only know that we all face evil in our lives at some point and there are people throughout the world who are led by evil and Marie faced it, lived with it and overcame it, and she is a true witness to God in her life.

Rev Carol

*****

I found this book a very interesting although a rather sad account of a young girl's life. The story was gripping and very hard to put down once I started to read it.

My wife and I have known Marie personally for over 24 years. We knew a little of the abuse, Marie had suffered but we had no idea as to the full extent of it and we were both shocked at the atrocities, which she had to overcome and accept in fear.

Her story gives very deep insights into the everyday life of a large working class family in the 60s and 70s. Sadly Marie's story must have been repeated many times during the dark periods of silence throughout the UK before it became acceptable to report such incidents.

Times have changed for the better thanks to the work of charities like Child Line.

I would like to thank Marie for sharing her life story with us and I hope it will encourage other families and children to break their silence at a time, which is right, and to realise that there is help available if they can find the courage to seek it.

Reverend David Ward

About the Author

Marie was born in Nottingham to a working class family, she is the middle child of seven, three brothers older and one brother and two sisters younger. Marie went to William Crane School for girls, left school at fifteen and went to work as a machine operator at John Players & Sons in the factory where she stayed until she left to have her own baby at the age of thirty.

She grew up with love and respect for her family, until she was 8 years old then her life was to turn upside down with changes within her family unit, Marie's three younger siblings became her responsibility when her Mother began her fight with cancer, only a child herself she had to take on most of her mothers duties including those in the bedroom. No one knew how ill her Mother was to become over 5 years, when Marie was still only 10 years old Marie's life took the brunt of it along with one of her brothers who was just 11 months her senior.

Marie is a wonderful woman who has the most beautiful caring nature when I think how far she has come in her life it is a miracle in its self.

Marie's Father even controlled her from beyond the grave with help and determination she gained self-confidence which make her liked by all who meet her.

I remember Marie's words when her Father died she said, *"I am relieved he is dead! I feel like a butterfly that is about to spread it's wings I have been living in a cocoon of misery most of my life, I am now able to be a real person in my own right, I had my childhood taken away, he will not take my whole life I will not let him"*.

Lightning Source UK Ltd.
Milton Keynes UK
09 June 2010

155340UK00002B/2/P